Silver Investing 2022

Step by Step Guide to Investing for Beginners

This book is licensed for your personal enjoyment only. This ebook may not be re-sold or given away to other people. If you would like to share this book with another person, please purchase an additional copy for each recipient. If you're reading this book and did not purchase it, or it was not purchased for your use only, then please return to Smashwords.com and purchase your own copy. Thank you for respecting the hard work of this author.

This eBook is Copyright © 2022. All Rights Reserved.

No part of this eBook may be reproduced or transmitted in any form or by any means, electronic or mechanical, including photocopying, recording, or by an information storage and retrieva system.

All trademarks and service marks are the properties of their respective owners. All references to these properties are made solely for editorial purposes. Except for marks actually owned by the Author, the Author (as both author and as publisher) does not make any commercial claims to their use, and is not affiliated with them in any way.

Table of Contents

Limits of Liability and Disclaimer of Warranties

Introduction – Why Silver Is the New Golden Investment Opportunity

1. From Pinching Pennies to a Six-figure Portfolio in Just Three Years

2. Forget What You Think You Know Now – The New Rules of Money

2.1. 1931 – The Birth of the Fed and Beginning of the End

2.2. 1971 – Nixon's Gambit and the Death of the Gold Standard

2.3. The Rabbit and the Hat –Government and Fed Perform an Old Trick

2.4. Fractured Finance – Fractional Reserve Banking

2.5. From Something to Nothing – Your Money Now

2.6. Daisies and Dollars – Beautiful to Look At, Impossible to Eat

2.7. Plastic Wealth – Being in Debt Forever Based on an Illusion

3. The Time Is Right For Precious Metal Investment Profits

3.1. Silver Is the New Gold

3.2. Silver Works in the Real World

3.3. Gold and Silver Have a Long History Together

3.4. The Limitations of Gold

3.5. Gold and Silver Provide the Best Defense

4. The Story of Silver and Why It Is A Better Choice Than Gold

4.1. Silver Is More Than Precious

4.2. Silver Is on the Bargain Table

4.3. Silver Is Used and Abused

4.4. Silver Is the Happy Child of an Essential Industry

4.5. Silver Production Is Low

4.6. The Gold and Silver Relationship – Can I Have the Next Dance?

4.7. From Grandma's Photograph to Heart Monitors

4.8. Silver's Love Affair with Electrons

5. How You Can Make a Fortune Investing in Silver

5.1. Timing, Markets, and Value – Looking Good Right Now

5.2. The Twenty Year Cycle and Silver

5.3. Housing Silver Long Term and Short Term

5.4. Silver ETFs in the Digital Age

5.5. Leveraging ETF AGQ for More Gain

5.6. Silver Numismatics – Not Just a Coin Toss

5.7. Silver Collectors – The Rare Made Valuable

5.8. Silver Mining Stocks – Don't Dig for Dollars

6. Seven Steps to Creating A Successful Investor Mindset

6.1. How to Crash and Burn with Instant Gratification

6.2. Avoiding a Rigged Game

6.3. Personal Responsibility Equals Success

6.4. The Long Haul

6.5. Skin Your Knees, Bruise Your Elbow, Get Back on that Bike!

6.6. It's All About Plot, Character Development, and Self-understanding

6.7. Grok It Fully Before You Go for It

6.8. Keep Teaching the Dog for Laughs and Giggles

6.9. It Seems Like an Eternity

6.10. A Little Thing Called Your Financial IQ

7. The Nuts And Bolts of Buying and Selling Silver

7.1. Margins and Leverage Accounts – Taming Calculated Risk 101

7.2. Taming Calculated Risk 102

7.3. Day Trading Revealed

7.4. Pattern Trading Is a Balancing Act

7.5. When to Take It to the Bank

7.6. The No-no of Negative Profit

7.7. More Leverage with Option Trading

8. Powerful Silver Investment Strategies that Make You Money

8.1. Keeping the Purity of a Single Solid Approach

8.2. Taxes for the Short and Long Terms

8.3. Buying Strategy 101 – On the Way Down

8.4. Buying Strategy 102 – On the Way Up

8.5. The Rule of 21 – Buying Beer and Silver

8.6. Taming Calculated Risk 103

8.7. What Temperature Is Your Thermometer Reading Now?

8.8. Kicking Out the House Guest

8.9. Know When to Exit

9. The Next 10 Years - Predictions For The Global Economy

9.1. Sturm und Drang – The Thunder of the Next Ten Years

9.2. The Fat Lady Isn't About to Sing Yet

9.3. Nero Said Everything Was Just Peachy

9.4. A Casket for a Currency

9.5. Please Mister, Can You Spare a Hundred Bucks?

9.6. Leveling the Unlevel Playing Field with a World-wide Solution

9.7. Bye Bye White Picket Fence

Bonus - How to Start Building Wealth in 90 Days

Recommended Resources

Limits of Liability and Disclaimer of Warranties

The materials in this eBook are provided "as is" and without warranties of any kind either express or implied. The Author disclaims all warranties, express or implied, including, but not limited to, implied warranties of merchantability and fitness for a particular purpose.

The Author does not warrant that defects will be corrected, or that that the site or the server that makes this eBook available are free of viruses or other harmful components. The Author does not warrant or make any representations regarding the use or the results of the use of the materials in this eBook in terms of their correctness, accuracy, reliability, or otherwise. Applicable law may not allow the exclusion of implied warranties, so the above exclusion may not apply to you.

Under no circumstances, including, but not limited to, negligence, shall the Author be liable for any special or consequential damages that result from the use of, or the inability to use this eBook, even if the Author or his authorized representative has been advised of the possibility of such damages. Applicable law may not allow the limitation or exclusion of liability or incidental or consequential damages, so the above limitation or exclusion may not apply to you. In no event shall the Author's total liability to you for all damages, losses, and causes of action (whether in contract, tort, including but not limited to, negligence or otherwise) exceed the amount paid by you, if any, for this eBook.

Facts and information are believed to be accurate at the time they were placed in this eBook. All data provided in this eBook is to be used for information purposes only. The information contained within is not intended to provide specific legal, financial or tax advice, or any other advice whatsoever, for any individual or company and should not be relied upon in that regard. The services described are only offered in jurisdictions where they may be legally offered. Information provided is not all-inclusive, and is limited to information that is made available and such information should not be relied upon as all-inclusive or accurate.

Earnings and Income Disclaimer

You recognize and agree that the Author has made no implications, warranties, promises, suggestions, projections, representations or guarantees whatsoever to you about future prospects or earnings, or that you will earn any money, with respect to your purchase of this eBook, and that the Author has not authorized any such projection, promise, or representation by others.

Any earnings or income statements, or any earnings or income examples, are only estimates of what you might earn. There is no assurance you will do as well as stated in any examples. If you rely upon any figures provided, you must accept the entire risk of not doing as well as the information provided. This applies whether the earnings or income examples are monetary in nature or pertain to advertising credits which may be earned (whether such credits are convertible to cash or not).

There is no assurance that any prior successes or past results as to earnings or income (whether monetary or advertising credits, whether convertible to cash or not) will apply, nor can any prior successes be used, as an indication of your future success or results from any of the information, content, or strategies. Any and all claims or representations as to income or earnings (whether monetary or advertising credits, whether convertible to cash or not) are not to be considered as "average earnings".

Testimonials & Examples

Testimonials and examples in this eBook are exceptional results, do not reflect the typical purchaser's experience, do not apply to the average person and are not intended to represent or guarantee that anyone will achieve the same or similar results. Where specific income or earnings (whether monetary or advertising credits, whether convertible to cash or not), figures are used and attributed to a specific individual or business, that individual or business has earned that amount.

There is no assurance that you will do as well using the same information or strategies. If you rely on the specific income or earnings figures used, you must accept all the risk of not doing as well. The described experiences are atypical. Your financial results are likely to differ from those described in the testimonials.

Businesses and earnings derived therefrom involve unknown risks and are not suitable for everyone. You may not rely on any information presented in this eBook or otherwise provided by the Author, unless you do so with the knowledge and understanding that you can experience significant losses (including, but not limited to, the loss of any monies paid to purchase this eBook and/or any monies spent setting up, operating, and/or marketing your business activities, and further, that you may have no earnings at all (whether monetary or advertising credits, whether convertible to cash or not).

Any and all forward looking statements here or on any materials in this eBook are intended to express an opinion of earnings potential. Many factors will be important in determining your actual results and no guarantees are made that you will achieve results similar to the Author or anybody else, in fact no guarantees are made that you will achieve any results from the Author's ideas and techniques found in this eBook.

You are advised to do your own due diligence when it comes to making business decisions and should use caution and seek the advice of qualified professionals. You should check with your accountant, lawyer, or professional advisor, before acting on this or any information. You may not consider any examples, documents, or other content in this eBook or otherwise provided by the Author to be the equivalent of professional advice.

The Author assumes no responsibility for any losses or damages resulting from your use of any link, information, or opportunity contained in this eBook or within any other information disclosed by the Author in any form whatsoever.

Introduction

Why Silver Is the New Golden Investment Opportunity

The global economy is a mess. I really don't have to tell you that. Some people actually want us to believe that the recession is over. They are either joking or really have no idea what they are talking about. The rumors of recession having actually ended may, in fact, be mere propaganda designed to keep this leaky balloon called our economy from releasing too much hot air too soon. Don't get me wrong. The movers and shakers in this world have good reason to slow down or trying to prevent the balloon from bursting. An overblown dollar that pops too quickly can spell disaster for everyone, not just the movers and shakers.

If you own a business, especially in retail, you know that the recession is actually getting worse. You know your costs and your likely margins. You know that your competitors are scrambling just as much as you are. You know your customers. There simply is not a lot of spending going on at any level. Multiply that by an entire nation, an entire global economy, and it spells real problems that cannot simply be smiled away by politicians and the talking heads on the six o'clock evening news.

On a personal level, it means that your financial security is in peril due to the changes – often catastrophic – that are rippling down from the world at large. Prepared or not, change is about to happen to everyone – big time.

I will tell you this up front: in economic, social, environmental and many other terms, we are all in for the biggest ride in history. What you see right now is just the tip of the iceberg. You can compare some events in U.S. history with the Titanic. When she was built she was the biggest luxury cruise ship in the world. She was built with pride using the best materials available. She was touted as the safest, most luxurious vessel afloat.

People were confident that she could take on the worst weather, push her way through the biggest icebergs and endure through any calamity the seas could throw at her. However, the Titanic was flawed from the very beginning, and it was that initial weakness in her design that ultimately led to her sinking.

Similarly to the story of the Titanic, very proud and intelligent persons in the U.S., along with some equally self-serving advice from their European banking counterparts, engineered a marvel of finance on a grand scale. In 1913 the Fed, which is nothing more than a cartel of private bankers that control the money supply, was sold to an unsuspecting public and their representatives. An extension of the idea of centralized banking systems that had seen development in almost all western countries during the 18th and 19th centuries, the Fed was seen by many at the time as the stalwart captain at the helm of the ship of money and finance. The Fed has now run into just the tip of an iceberg that will ultimately sink the U.S. economy and take other economies along with it. Like the Titanic, the Fed has a fatal flaw, possibly the biggest in the history of the United States. Like the Titanic, the Fed's makers and captains have realized only too late the nature of their hubris around this flaw when it comes to navigating the behemoth U.S. economy to safe harbors around the world.

A second flaw was created in our economy in 1974 when President Nixon convinced the senate to abandon the gold standard, and to push the rest of the world to make the dollar the global trading currency. Together, the creation of the Fed and the abandonment of the gold standard are the cornerstones of our current financial disaster. You will learn more about these two pivotal events in a following chapter.

In 1912 the world learned of the horrific tragedy of the Titanic's sinking, a disaster that claimed more than 1,500 lives. In 2008 we all were witness to how the olympian U.S. economy hit its own iceberg and began its startling descent, pulling hundreds of thousands of individuals and businesses into the vortex along with it. The death toll for this disaster has yet to be fully determined. We now know that the U.S. economy had been perilously close to sinking for some time, by the estimates of some experts a matter of hours away from total bankruptcy, kept afloat only by 'lifeboats' of dollars printed out of nothing more substantial than air.

Like the dot com bubble before it, the housing bubble of 2006 had burst, this time with even more far-reaching consequences. The lifeboats can only go so far. Sooner, rather than later, the U.S. economy will ultimately lose its remaining buoyancy and nothing in the world can stop its plunge to the depths.

When the U.S. economy does sink it will negatively impact all major industrialized countries even more than before. The initial bump into the iceberg as just a hint of what is in store for the world at large. No one anywhere in the world will be immune from the tsunami created with so many economic vessels on their way to oblivion. There are no lifeboats large enough to withstand a wave of economic destruction on that scale. Nevertheless, readers of this book can benefit from the information found within no matter what their nationality or place of birth.

Never before in human history have we relied on the titanic structure of one economy to serve as the bellwether for the entire global market. It was only recently in relative terms that the global marketplace had begun to function as an interconnected whole rather than as a bucket of bolts. Our global financial perspective was one of calm seas and clear skies, enabled by advances in electronic market reporting with billions of transactions taking place in just microseconds. Staggering amounts of money are landing in far-flung ports around the world with precision and certainty much like cargo during our grandfathers' time made its way from one exotic locale to another around the world.

However, our grandfathers' markets were a different order of magnitude altogether. The effects of modern investment and banking vehicles, coupled with nearly instantaneous exchange of untold wealth, mean potentially great windfalls as well as disastrous shortfalls. Modern investment vehicles are complex and designed to work quickly. Some are much riskier than others. Many are not well understood by those who are in positions of countering challenges to the economy. Many, through no inherent fault of their own, play to people's greed and disregard. All this can be wrapped up in one word: derivatives.

A derivative, if you are not familiar with this term, is simply anything that derives from a service or product. So orange juice would be a derivative of oranges and a mortgage is a derivative of a house. In the world of finance, swaps, futures and options are all types of derivatives. By its definition, a financial derivative is based on the value of some expected future price.

The dollar amount of the various financial derivatives that are floating around most likely exceeds $100 trillion dollars, which is equal to a one with fourteen zeros after it: 100,000,000,000,000. To give you a better idea of this number lets compare it with some other things.

- There are probably 150 Billion galaxies in the universe,

- About 200 Billion stars in the Milky Way

- And 100 Trillion is the estimated number of cells in the entire human body

One way to better understand large numbers such as these is to compare the heights of stacks of varying numbers of dollar bills. The thickness of a single one dollar bills measures .0043 inches or .0000000679 miles.

The height of a stack of 100,000,000 (one hundred million) one dollar bills measures 35,851 feet or 6.79 miles. This would reach from the earth's surface to the approximate altitude at which commercial jetliners fly.

The height of a stack of 100,000,000,000 (one hundred billion) one dollar bills measures 6,786.6 miles. A column of bills this high would extend 28 times higher than the orbiting International Space Station.

The height of a stack of 1,000,000,000,000 (one trillion) one dollar bills measures 67,866 miles. This would reach more than one fourth the way from the earth to the moon.

The height of a stack of 100,000,000,000,000 (one hundred trillion) one dollar bills measures 6,786,616 miles. This would reach from the earth to the moon – and back – 14 times.

No GDP figures have been published since 2008. In basic terms, GDP is defined as a measure of a country's overall economic output. It is the market value of all final goods and services made within the borders of a country in a year.

This clearly illustrates the problem when you compare it to the gross domestic product (GDP) of the U.S. which was $14 trillion in 2008. Just to let you know how significant this number is, it includes the associated healthcare costs of all sick people in the U.S. as well. This figure alone does not distinguish whether or not a product or service is sustainable or contributes to wealth. For example: very single cent for war counts toward productivity factored into the GDP. So the real number, a healthy number not involving real contributing productivity would be far less than the reported $14 trillion.

What that illustrates is that the GDP is, in effect, not only inflated by some indeterminate amount due to the inclusion of nonproductive economic factors, the dollar is weaker in real terms than everyone would like to believe. Pointing to a $14 trillion GDP as a sign of inherent strength becomes meaningless in real world terms, particularly when economic crises are brewing in all economies around the world.

While there is not much you can hope to achieve as an individual on these macro-economic scales, there is one thing you can do as an individual to help protect your money and even profit from it during these times: get yourself a good financial education that clearly helps you put the historic process into perspective so you can make good financial decisions today and tomorrow.

There are two forms of investments you can make. Either you invest in capital gain or in cash flow. Either one can work – it is even better to invest in both. This book will teach you how to invest in silver and create massive capital gain. If you use this profit wisely you may want to re-invest it for cash flow. There is nothing more satisfying than seeing your bank account filled up as if by magic by the beginning of each month without having to do any work. However hard you worked in the past, you no longer have to work. It does not get much better than that!

That's when the real pleasure sets in and you can enjoy your life without any financial stress. And if you have smartened up enough during your financial education, you have learned how to handle the tax issues – so no more worries about taxes as well. At this point in your life you can shift your focus from working for working's sake to being creative. That's when you go for your dreams.

In the first chapters of this book you will dig a bit into the history of money. How will learn how money, something that manages to be both immaterial and substantial at the same time, actually springs into existence. Those parents among you have probably been asked by your children at one time or another to explain where money comes from. I guess you told them that it gets printed, which is actually true for 5 percent of everything we call money. Little bits of printed paper do not really explain how it all actually works.

Finding out about how money is actually created will be a big eye opener for you. It may startle you, delight you, even awaken you to an infinite range of possibility for abundance and security you could only imagine in the past. If you already know the mechanics of the birth of money, you can still further your financial education along with the rest of us by delving into why silver is arguably the best investment opportunity anywhere right now.

We are all currently witnessing the dismantling of a vast empire. Perhaps it will be the last empire. Perhaps that will be a good indication that humanity has outgrown the need for empires of all kinds. The juggernaut of the United States has passed the point of no return in monetary terms; the national debt is now so huge that it must go into either default or into hyperinflation to cope with the growing disparities found in its financial markets and banking system. Either option is dire and nearly impossible to recover from without massive systemic restructuring on all fronts.

The demise of the dollar will not be the first time that a currency has collapsed. When you thoroughly look into the historical record, currencies and money systems have always ultimately collapsed. In fact, this has happened every single time. The type of currency we have right now – called fiat money – is the same type that the overwhelming majority of the entire world has in one form or another. Fiat money has a 100 percent failure rate. Throughout history, in all cultures great and small, every fiat currency ends up with a real value of absolutely zero.

Think of what that will me to you and your family when all those hard-earned dollars you have in the bank are worthless and any dollars you earn tomorrow are likewise without value. You will need a crash course in Economics 101 without the hyperbole and misdirection that are so prevalent in today's financial world. It is my hope that you will agree with me that investing in silver is an excellent way to stave off future economic uncertainty and protect your wealth.

If you're like me, you will want to dive in right now and start making money with silver. However, I strongly encourage you to read the first few chapters of this book to gain a better understanding of the world economy. With such knowledge you can move forward with confidence knowing that you have a solid foundation upon which to base your upcoming trading strategies.

In the next chapter you will learn why silver is actually a much better investment than gold. Most individual investors and the financial press are biased toward gold while seeing silver as a secondary investment in precious metals. You will see why this is not the case and learn how to use silver's under-the-radar status to your advantage.

Next, you'll jump right into the physical metal itself and how it is quite likely that silver will become the first of our metals that become extinct. You will learn why silver is rarer than gold, and why it has not yet caught up with its real price value. You will come to understand why most silver ends up in the land fill, why falling silver demand due to reduced photographic usage is a myth, and how silver is used in countless technical processes in all kinds of industries. These technologies, in fact, have driven the demand for silver so high that we no longer have a large surplus of the metal available to help balance the market during times of scarcity.

The next chapter deals with the different ways to acquire silver in both physical and paper forms. You will get the details on why silver is remains undervalued and how the fundamental market outlook for silver will be bullish for the coming next few years at least.

After that we are going into the nuts and bolts of trading. You will learn how to trade silver to create the highest profit. You will learn how to use and apply several stages of leverage, which will exponentially increase your return on investment. You will learn techniques to substantially reduce your risk when buying with leverage. You will be amazed how much money you can make in a short amount of time in the current bull market.

Speaking of leverage, it is a myth that more leverage equates to increased risk. This myth is of the same type as the one about diversifying as a means of spreading risk. You only need to diversify if you don't know what you're doing. Likewise, you can count on greater risk when leveraging if you don't know what you're doing. The Silver Fortune Formula methods are based on minimizing risk. We'll show you how to achieve this. When you fully understand the fundamentals of an investment – and know how to minimize risk – you can simply and confidently make up your mind to jump in or to leave it alone.

In the next chapter you will learn the basic general principles of being a successful investor. It all begins with mental preparation and knowing how to turn your mind into an asset. Once your mind is asset the particulars of your worldly physical existence will unfold in the same way. This is actually the most important and crucial chapter because it assures you success forever. You may at a certain time in your life be broke, but you will never be poor. Being poor is only a state of mind, being broke is only temporary.

In the final chapter you will get an overview of the global economy and get an idea of where the global economy is going. This information will be important for developing strategies to protect your investments. Our recession (and possible coming depression) is really only the tip of the iceberg for the ship of the U.S. economy. Things will get worse for quite some time before we begin to see the beginnings of a better, more resilient global economy to take its place.

The current financial system is broken and does not support us any longer. It is not a question of if it will fail – it is a question of when it will happen. If you educate yourself now, you will be prepared for the cascade of changes to come and learn how to benefit from the largest transfer of wealth the world has ever seen. It's really a simple black and white question that involves deciding to be poor or to be wealthy. I assume that you already made up your mind; otherwise you would not have acquired this book.

Last but not least, a word about learning. Your financial education will be tremendously more successful if you learn to roll with the punches. Don't give yourself a hard time when you have trouble grasping a term or understanding a method illustrated in this book. Our system of education, like all our other systems, is pretty much in the same bad shape as our economy. Industrial age educational principles with an emphasis on conformity and rote memorization were designed to produce workers with little initiative and creative problem solving skills, not flexible, self-aware individuals who can confidently assimilate new concepts and put them to use. The best investors learn in this fashion and so too will you.

You will experience hiccups here and there during your personal financial education. Slow down if you need to, cultivate patience with yourself, and soon you will see that learning can actually be a fun thing. When you are engaged and curious about the subject material and calm enough to see emerging possibilities, learning will not be an issue at all.

In this book you will learn two things:

1. Silver is a fantastic investment instrument

2. Silver investment tactics to make huge profits

Chapter 1

From Pinching Pennies to a Six-figure Portfolio In Just Three Years

"Do not wait until the conditions are perfect to begin. Beginning makes the conditions perfect." - Alan Cohen

Four years ago my wife and I moved from Hawaii to California. Many people asked us why we would leave such a wonderful place like Hawaii. The answer is simple – we needed change. As wonderful and indulging Hawaii can be, if you live anywhere for several years, even in paradise, you may come to no longer appreciate what you have. That happened to us and we soon began to want to start something new. Our new dream life would involve some sort of business that could help people achieve prosperity and abundance in their lives.

We arrived in California with two suitcases each and a few thousand dollars in our savings account. As we didn't know where we wanted to live, we cruised around for several months living in cheap motels as we explored different areas. Our savings dwindled quickly and we decided to switch to renting a room in areas that we wanted to check out more thoroughly. That turned out to be a good decision as we met more people and spent less on room and board.

It was during the time The Secret had come out and we loved it. We loved it so much that some of its ideas sparked the creation of our own vision board as a way to give substance to our dreams. Our first idea was to do an actual physical version of a vision board but we soon realized that this would be very limiting so we decided to create a software application that would allow anyone to create one on their computer.

We were excited. We finally had an idea and we started to pour all our energy and effort into it. Lots of decisions had to be made. We founded Dream Manifesto, LLC and started to build a website. I worked day and night and sometimes I had so many obstacles to overcome that I didn't know where my head was anymore.

I do have some knowledge of computers and electronics; however, I had not a clue how to begin creating what was needed for an electronic vision board. Where to begin? I studied programming techniques for days only to get endless error messages on my screen. Many times I was ready to call it quits. But slowly I made some small progress and things started to work out.

We moved into a small apartment complex and spent our weekends going to garage sales to get our new home furnished. Ah, the joys of having a bed, a table to eat on and some desks to work on. At that stage we were quickly running out of funds so we started to make calls to friends and relatives to borrow money. Every month we did not have one penny in income but we did have about $3,000 in expenses. It was very challenging to come up with the money each time; however, we were excited about what we were doing and dreaming about doing and knew that things would work out eventually.

After only five months we were able to break even and did not need to borrow any more money. I remember the day we finished including the online payment option on the website. We waited in anticipation for the first order to come in. It did soon enough, and by the end of the day, we had a total of five. We were so happy – it was a huge success for us.

A friend of ours recommended that we customize our e-mail client to play a specific sound when an order came in. I decided to go for an applause. From then on every time we got an order we got a huge round of applause to cheer us up. It was like getting a shot of adrenaline where we needed it most.

Back in Hawaii I had started to read some financial books. I remember how awkward I felt when I had picked up my first book on getting rich. I certainly had a lot of beliefs and concepts around this topic both pro and con. My middle class upbringing did little to instill a sense of excitement about the possibility of becoming wealthy. My parents both worked for the government and strongly believed in good education and hard work. Success was measured in very small doses and in years of toil – any other approach was seen as a mere pipe dream.

At that time it was all about saving money and living on a budget. I remember that my parents sat together in conference once every week to go over the monthly budget. My mother used paper envelopes to hold the amount of money she was allowed to spend for different things. My father also got his monthly allowance and I always wondered how he could ever be satisfied with the little money he got.

In one of the first get rich books I encountered a new radical idea. The concept of paying yourself first. That was a slap to my face as I never ever had considered paying myself first. Money came in and immediately went to the most pressing bills and expenses first, and anything left over was good enough. However, I learned quickly that if you don't follow this pattern, you will never have anything to invest. It took a while to understand that all investing comes from what you can pay yourself first, not something that may or may not be left over from paying others first. The truth of the matter was, I seldom had any money left over for investing in my future even during the times I earned a lot. I had trained myself to spend it all, updating my living situation or car or something else and by the end of the month, there was indeed nothing left in my account to save or invest.

Like most people, I also strongly held the belief that saving (investing) money is not a good idea because it does not allow for instant gratification, which seemed to me to be a cornerstone of personal happiness. I was basically doing nothing more than reacting to my parents' own financial belief system. For them it was all about saving so I just did the opposite – I spent everything. I felt very good about it – I really believed this is it – I am on the right track.

Finally I realized that without paying myself first, there would never be enough money left in my account to save and invest. More realizations popped into my head. I also came to the conclusion that time is limited and that if I based by work on getting paid by the hour, my income would always be likewise limited. That definitely did not felt good. Imagine making only what you can command in terms of the hours you spend on the job! There had to be a better way. There was, and this turned out to be an excellent reason to invest the time needed to establish an online business that allows us to replicate a product instantly without further demands. In this way, time is invested wisely once but has big payoffs that quickly multiply the return on this investment. The idea is pure genius. No wonder Bill Gates made billions with it. There is basically no limit on how times you can exactly replicate a given program and that means there is no limit to your income.

Paying ourselves first was the most crucial and important step into shifting our mindset. It was the start of financial education and I see now after five years of intensive research on this topic that getting a solid financial education is one of the most important tasks an intelligent person can undertake.

Being financially educated means that we now make more money from our investment accounts than from our business income. Our next step will be to convert some of these cash flow incomes into assets that pay us residual income over time. It was in our initial search of these residual income options that we came to understand how all the pieces of the money puzzle had fallen into place.

So why am I telling your our story? We want to help you create your own success story by understanding ours. Very simply, we probably had fewer start-up resources than you have right now. You are probably in a better position than we were when we started. But sometimes the oddest things can turn out to be wonderful resources. You see, I may have a slight advantage over you in an unexpected way. I was kicked out of school when I was 18 years old. Why would that be an advantage? Simply because I have had the benefit of a few more years of creative freedom when it comes to problem solving and a few less years of the rigid indoctrination each of us undergoes in the public education system. Perhaps I ended up with less garbage to clear out of my head. Perhaps I had fewer filters that imposed limiting beliefs on my mindset.

In any event, I learned sooner than most that for any good idea to become successful in the world, a certain amount of original thinking as well as some dissatisfaction were both essential ingredients in getting those ideas out into the world where they could do the most good for myself and for others.

After my first internship with a major electronic company I realized rather quickly that continuing along this avenue would not bring me happiness and satisfaction in life. Even getting another two years of education in electronics and computer science, things I really enjoyed, would not guarantee me solid employment let alone rapid advancement. Realizing this, I started my first company when I was in electronics school.

If you are employed or even self-employed your income is limited and you are also in a high tax bracket. The goal is to become a business owner and an investor. Both distinguish themselves from the usual employment roles by providing potential capital gains and cash flow, things employment alone cannot provide.

In the following chapters I will help you lay the groundwork for preparing yourself to take advantage of one of the biggest transfer of wealth transfers in human history. You can be part of it and create huge capital gains. It will require a certain ability to take a chance now and then, a solid education in how the marketplace functions, a commitment to learn from your mistakes and a deep understanding in your own strengths and ability to handle change. The middle class will soon be wiped out and you need to make a choice if you want to be poor or rich. If you do not make that decision it is high likely you will end up being poor because the decision will be made for you.

Chapter 2

Forget What You Think You Know Now – The New Rules of Money

"The process by which banks create money is so simple that the mind is repelled."

—John Kenneth Galbraith

This first chapter may be shocking and disturbing to you. You may feel your stomach in knots by the time you have finished reading it. You will come to understand that money is no longer really money at all but something that has been turned into worthless, debt-ridden currency. Pull out your wallet and take a look at bill. Whether it's a dollar or ten or a twenty, it has no longer intrinsic value. It is nothing other than debt, which you owe to someone else, like it or not. The banknote you hold in your hand is not even worth the few pennies the ink costs to print it.

It's time for a paradigm shift in your perceptions around money. It's a powerful story, this tale of how our money came to be worthless. It may take you a few days to digest this information and to understand the true consequences of what has happened. Read this entire chapter as often as you need. Do not read further until you have grasped the concept of what has happened to your money.

2.1 1931 – The Birth of the Fed and Beginning of the End

It may come as a surprise to you to learn that the Federal Reserve is not the original Central Bank of the United States. In fact, it is really the third Central Bank in the history of the U.S. The First Bank of the United States existed from 1791 to 1811. The Second Bank of the United States had a similar 20 year reign from 1816 to 1836.

Both banks engaged in commercial loans, took in deposits, issued currency, and bought securities. The two banks also contained a number of regional branches and performed fiscal agent duties on behalf of the United States Treasury. The biggest difference between these first two central banks and the Federal Reserve Bank lay in the fact that these other two central banks were 80 percent privately held, with stockholders voting for 80 percent of the banks' directors.

As a result of a long standing series of financial panics and economic instabilities that culminated in the financial panic of 1907, the United States looked into creating a more stable Central Bank in the years of 1912 to 1913. There was much opposition and great debate within Congress, but the Federal Reserve Act at last passed just before the Christmas recess in 1913.

A system of twelve regional banks had been enacted in order to spread the authority of the Central Bank out between the East coast and the rest of the country. Despite this, the New York Fed became the first among equals in the new system. It maintains several privileges to this day, including engaging in open market operations as instructed by the Federal Reserve Open Market Committee.

The rise of the Federal Reserve Bank to prominence began almost immediately after its starting operations in 1915. Its first major accomplishment lay in its function in a critical role as financier of both the American and the Allied war efforts in the First World War. From this humble beginning, the Federal Reserve has only risen to greater prominence and importance in the U.S. economy and eventually that of the world.

The Federal Reserve began acquiring greater powers in the depths of the Great Depression. They began setting interest rates for the nation in an effort to influence economic growth and intervene in the severity of economic downturns. This power was never relinquished, and is one that they maintain and use aggressively to this day.

During World War II, the Federal Reserve had to surrender some of its powers by agreeing not to raise interest rates on Treasury Bills above 0.375 percent. This compromise was made in an effort to support the war efforts, which it did heroically even after the Allies won the war. Afterward, in 1951, the Federal Reserve signed The Accord with the U.S. Treasury and regained its independence.

The Breton-Woods Agreement proved to be the turning point for the Fed in becoming an agency that had an impact on all economies of the world. This arrangement following World War II set up a new global reserve system with the reserve currency based on the dollar. This meant that the Fed's actions in raising and lowering interest rates now influenced the policies and currencies of all countries in the world.

In the 1970's the Fed became obsessed with the mission of battling down inflation. Inflation had risen to out of hand levels throughout the decade, and the Federal Reserve chairman Paul Volcker made it his goal to get it under control. The Fed actually fought inflation by targeting bank reserves, another power it assumed in its march towards controlling the economy. They were so successful at this that by 1987, inflation was down to a mere percent, from its highs in the mid double digits of the 1970's.

The Federal Reserve continues to exercise its muscles to this day. In the early years of the new century, from 2001 to 2003, they lowered interest rate thirteen times to fight recessions. From 2004 to 2006, the Fed then raised interest rates seventeen consecutive times.

In March of 2006, the Federal Reserve unilaterally decided to stop giving out the most accurate means of measuring the money supply anymore, known as M3. With this powerful act, they had completed their destiny of growing from a limited powers organization to becoming one that could set interest rates, determine individual bank reserves, and even dictate the ways that they shared information on their activities of increasing or reducing money supply of the U.S. dollar that impacted the entire world economy.

2.2 1971 – Nixon's Gambit and the Death of the Gold Standard

Another real change that shook the U.S. financial system and dollar proved to be President Nixon's decision to take the U.S. dollar off of the long standing gold standard. Contrary to what you may believe, he did not turn out to be the first major economy to do this. West Germany and Switzerland were actually the first two countries to withdraw from the Breton-Woods agreement governing the gold standard and international currency exchange.

The United States made the decision to follow suit for several reasons. On the one hand, the rising spending of the government on both domestic programs and the Vietnam War caused the country to realize its first trade deficit and balance of payments deficit in the entire twentieth century. This marked a critical point in the country's modern finances, as the Austrian School of economics and the Neoclassical economists argue that at this point, countries and individual holders of the dollar gave up on their belief in the government's ability to reduce trade deficits and its budget.

Because of this, other countries and investors were exchanging their dollars for gold at a shocking rate. Gold coverage pertaining to paper dollars fell by thirty-three points from 55 to 22 percent in only the single year of 1970. As the country continued to print a great number of dollars with which to cover the country's military bills and domestic spending, more and more gold found its way from the U.S. Treasury to other countries, who surrendered their paper dollars for gold. France and Switzerland proved to be extremely aggressive in their withdrawal of gold for dollars. France drew down fifty million while Switzerland demanded one hundred and ninety-one million dollars in gold.

The dollar began to drop sharply against other major world currencies like the Deutschmark and the other European countries' currencies. With this going on, West Germany withdrew from the international agreements. Switzerland followed suit three months later. Congress began recommending that the country devalue the dollar to defend it.

President Nixon responded with drastic actions. In order to help stabilize the economy, severe inflation, and the dollar, he enacted a series of dramatic moves. He put a ninety day price and wage freeze into effect, levied a ten percent import tax on imports, and ended the U.S. dollar's convertibility directly to gold. The

President and his advisors did this without consulting with the international monetary system representatives, giving it the informal name of the Nixon Shock.

At the time, President Nixon's policies proved to be very popular domestically. Members of the public gave him credit for saving American citizens from runaway inflation and price gougers. He received accolades for staving off the foreign exchange crisis as well.

Internationally, this abandoning of the gold standard caused the Bretton-Woods agreement to totally collapse. By 1976, all of the important currencies in the world had moved to floating systems. The dollar's value no longer resided on a basis of gold value. It now floated based on the concept of an estimated potential future value.

The long term effects proved to be less desirable. Some economists and political scientists have claimed that the 2007 Great Recession developed as a result of the collapse of the Bretton-Woods agreement and the gold standard. This is because the failure of these arrangements led to a great amount of volatility in money and the creation of instruments that were not properly regulated or were even unregulated. Because of the greater volatility, a need arose for financial instruments that could hedge risk, like derivatives and credit default swaps. These complex off balance sheet arrangements were much credited with leading to the financial meltdown of 2007.

2.3 The Rabbit and the Hat – The Government and the Fed Perform an Old Trick

You will likely find it hard to believe that the government, through the Federal Reserve, is actually able to create money out of thin air. This concept has been referred to in the ancient and medieval world as ex nihilo, or out of nothing. This creation of money from nothing is not only possible today, but it is a commonly accepted and pursued policy.

Listen to the words of Federal Reserve Bank Chairman Benjamin Bernake, if you doubt the truth of this statement. He said in 2002 that the United States government possesses a modern day technology of an electronic equivalent to the printing press that permits it to create all of the U.S. dollars that it wants.

He made later statements about this printing of money that earned him the nickname of Helicopter Ben, when he claimed that if the U.S. economy ever ran into real difficulties, then he could salvage it if he only had a large enough helicopter to fly around the country throwing out bales of this money that was created out of nothing to the citizens.

Bernake is a professor whose specialty dealt with the Great Depression. His statements regarding the country's capability of electronically printing money from thin air may be controversial. You will see below that the truth is that they have evolved into a main component of the American economy in the twenty-first century.

You have to comprehend how modern money works in order to internalize how a modern day electronic printing press is able to make money from nothing. The actual currency of the U.S. does not prove to be the Federal Reserve dollars that move around the United States and its economy. Instead, the real currency turns out to be Treasury bonds and bills that are backed up by faith and credit of the government.

People, investors, and countries who hold these U.S. Treasuries receive the only guarantee of being paid by the government from taxes that will be collected from American citizens in the future. This guarantee to treasury holders is what really underlies what you use as money in the form of dollar bills.

Fortunately for the U.S. government, the U.S. treasuries' market remains the deepest and most liquid on earth. This makes it easy for the Fed and the government to conjure new dollars out of thin air. The Fed does this by simply monetizing the debt of the government. In other words, the Fed will step into the open markets and purchase Treasuries.

When they do this, they do not pay with real dollars to the seller of the Treasuries. Instead, they simply credit the account of the seller for the action. This proves to be Bernake's electronic equivalent that he had mentioned in his earlier speech. You are right to think that the value credited to the account of the seller does not literally exist. It is merely an on screen balance of the bank's reserves with the Fed.

With these actions of monetizing the debt, the Federal Reserve has actually printed money from nothing. They are able to do this so long as the Treasuries market remains so deep and liquid. The transaction also requires sufficient confidence to be present that the seller will accept the crediting of its account by the Federal Reserve. Until either of these two underlying pinnacles is called into question, then the Federal Reserve and the government will continue to have the ability to literally create money electronically out of nothing through monetizing the government's debt.

You may be asking yourself a good question now. If the government creates money from thin air, would this not affect the value of the entire dollar money supply, both that already exists and that they are creating? The answer to the question is a resounding yes. Later in this chapter you will see start to see how this magical printing of money actually has negative consequences for the demand and value of the U.S. dollar.

2.4 Fractured Finance – Fractional Reserve Banking

This creating money by monetizing the government's debt is not the only way that the Fed is able to create new dollars. They can also use the Fractional Reserve Banking System that underpins the modern banking of practically all countries in the world.

Fractional reserve banking significantly expands the money supply, or demand deposits and cash, beyond the level at which it would normally be. Because of how common the practice of fractional reserve banking proves to be, the actual money supply found in the majority of nations is a multiple bigger than only the base level of money that a nation's Central Bank creates.

The multiple itself is known as the money multiplier. This number is set by the minimum reserve requirement that the financial regulatory authorities require and impose on banks. Extra reserves that banks hold also influence the level of this multiple.

You will find that most central banks, including the Federal Reserve, generally set these minimum reserve requirements for the banks. This ensures that banks maintain at least a minimal amount of their on demand deposits in cash reserves. In such a way, the money creation performed in the commercial banking realm is controlled by the Central Bank or Federal Reserve.

This is also intended to make certain that banks possess sufficient available on hand cash to deal with typical withdrawal demands. Even though these fractional reserve minimums are intended to prevent them, difficulties can become evident if a great number of bank depositors attempt to pull out their money at once. This leads to bank runs on rare occasions. If the problems are exaggerated to banks throughout a region or are severe, it can also cause a systemic crisis in the banking system.

To help alleviate these types of difficulties and protect the system, the Federal Reserve oversees and closely regulates such commercial banks. It furthermore functions as a true lender of last resort for them. Besides this, another body, the FDIC, or Federal Deposit Insurance Corporation, insures commercial bank customers' deposits.

Because banks are allowed to lend out a certain multiple of the deposits that they actually have, they can be utilized by the Federal Reserve to create additional money. You have already seen that they can lend out a multiple of the deposits that they have on hand. Another way of putting this is that the Federal Reserve only requires them to keep a certain percentage of loans that they make as reserves.

Typically, this fractional reserve number is ten percent. This means that for every $1 that they have in reserves, a bank is allowed to loan out $10. They are given a money multiplier of ten to one with this reserve.

So when the Fed purchases Treasuries by crediting a financial institution's account, they are electronically increasing the reserves' value of the bank in question. The bank is then not simply able to loan out these deposits that are magically credited to them digitally, but instead the full fractional reserve multiplier of what is typically ten to one. This means that the Federal Reserve creates not only the money that they use to purchase treasuries with, but also the ten to one in new money that is created by a bank loaning out up to their fractional reserve requirements.

Every modern bank in the United States operates on this system of fractional reserve lending. This whole explanation may come as a shock to you, as it does to most Americans when they learn of it. Reality is that far more money is loaned out than the banks literally keep in reserves. Although there are restrictions to how much money the banks can create, you have already seen that the restrictions are mostly limited to the ten percent fractional reserve requirement.

Should the Federal Reserve Bank desire it, they can lower the reserve still further, allowing yet more money to be created as if by magic from thin air. This has profound implications for your money and its value. Later in the chapter we will examine what this means for you and your paper and electronic dollars.

2.5 From Something to Nothing – Your Money Now

In the good old days of the 1800s through 1971, money proved to be as good as gold. This is because until Nixon took the United States off of the gold standard, money was literally exchangeable for gold. This led to an incredibly stable period in the value of the dollar and other major world currencies that lasted for literally more than a hundred and fifty years.

When you look at the value of the dollar against gold from 1792 to1862 when the Civil War had begun, you see that gold closed each year in that seventy year period in the range of $19.39 per ounce to $21.60 per ounce. You witnessed a deviation of no more than 11 percent in the value of gold and hence the dollar in seventy years. Another way of putting this is that in seventy years, the dollar had only declined around 11 percent against fixed asset gold. Similarly after the Civil War ended and recovery ensued, from 1870 to 1932 the dollar against gold remained steady around $20 to $22 per ounce. This proved to be another more than sixty year period where the dollar had no more than a ten percent deviation in value.

Money started its gradual descent to increasingly worthless currency when the government began to play with the gold standard. The first real instance of this proved to be in 1933 when President Franklin Roosevelt decided to intentionally devalue the dollar against gold. When he declared gold to be worth $35 per ounce against the dollar, he started a depreciation that caused the dollar to fall almost 70 percent from the closing values in 1932 to 1934. It did not matter that the President did this intentionally. This proved to be the biggest single decline in the dollar in its history to that point.

Still, the gold standard last another forty years for the United States, and so long as the government did not interfere with the dollar gold convertibility, the dollar held its value remarkably well once more. From 1935 to to 1971, gold closed every year in a range of $35 to $43.50. These were far more tumultuous years, but the dollar still held its own over the thirty six year period, declining by not even 25 percent despite the challenges of the Great Depression, World War II, and the Korean and Vietnam Wars.

The fatal moment for the dollar and other world currencies has already been described earlier in this chapter. President's Nixon's unilateral decision to withdraw from the gold standard started a stampede for the exits. The gold standard died an ignoble death over the next few years. This is exactly the point where currency value stability ended, in particular for the U.S. dollar.

From 1970 to 1983, the dollar dropped sharply against gold. It went from a 1970 closing value of $39 to a 1982 closing value of $447, at one point touching a mind blowing $850 per ounce. In thirteen years, the dollar, once a bedrock of stability and value, dropped 1,046 percent.

The fortunes of the dollars value waxed and waned with economic news and cycles from 1971 forward. The currency had become a paper instrument whose only value lay in the faith and credit of the U.S. government. This meant that the value would lie entirely in how creditworthy the U.S. economy and how trustworthy the U.S. government appeared from this point forward. In the years from the 1970 last year of the gold standard, to the prices as of the first of October 2010, the dollar has steadily declined in value over time, despite periodic bounces.

Today's dollar is valued at $1,320 dollars per ounce. Remember that this level has been reached from $39 per ounce in 1970. The last forty years have represented the most shocking collapse in the value of money in modern history. The dollar, and most of the other now paper currencies around the world, has plummeted a staggering 3,285 percent.

To put that in concrete terms for you, had you seen the writing on the wall regarding the gradual devaluation of paper currencies, you might have sunk your money into gold to maintain its real value. Your actual thousand dollars in 1970 would today be worth a mind numbing $32,846. This does not represent investment gains that you would have made in stocks, bond, real estate, or other speculative investments. It is simply how far the paper dollar has declined in value since it officially lost gold's blessing and backing forty years ago. Can there be any doubt as to paper money's gradual descent to worthless currency?

2.6 Daisies and Dollars – Beautiful to Look At, Impossible to Eat

You may be wondering at this point how it is possible that the dollar has fallen off a cliff to the tune of 3,285 percent in forty years. It is not as a result of the fall of the U.S. economy. Even though the country's economic leadership has taken its share of hard knocks in the last forty years, the U.S. economy remains unquestionably the largest and most vibrant in the entire world.

The other G7 countries of Japan, Germany, Great Britain, France, Italy, and Canada, plus China, when all combined, still do not surpass the United States' Gross Domestic Product, or total value of all goods and service produced in a year. The dollar's upsetting longer term value problem does not lie with the U.S. economy or credit rating, or any other single factor.

The dollar's problem stems from the fact that since President Nixon's monumental move in 1971, it no longer has any intrinsic value at all. You might be unclear on the notion of intrinsic value. The word intrinsic as described by Merriam Webster relates to a value that belongs to the constitution or essential nature of a thing.

Intrinsic pertains to the inner nature and worth of something based on its own merits. A diamond has intrinsic value because of its purity, quality, clarity, sparkle, and rarity. Similarly, gold has intrinsic value that results from its luster, color, historical worth, and rarity. But the dollar, or any other paper currency not backed up by gold, has nothing intrinsic to it. It is a simple piece of paper with colored ink on it. It is neither shiny nor glamorous looking. It is certainly not rare.

Instead the dollar's intrinsic value is now based on perception of its worth. This is much like the value of stocks and similar assets, whose values stem from the underlying perception of real value that is derived from every business aspect, both intangible and tangible in nature. You are probably asking yourself who decides the perception of the dollar's worth?

The international currency markets determine any currency's worth these days since the gold standard was abandoned. This is more or less done through market oriented forces of supply and demand. You know that demand for the dollar has remained strong over the decades. Even after the hits that it has taken, the dollar still remains the world's reserve currency for now, as it was back in the fifties, sixties, and seventies. If demand for the dollar continues to be strong, then what explains the 3,285 percent drop in its real value?

Part of the answer is the other side of the supply and demand side of the equation, supply. The government has a long history of printing more dollars year in and year out. President Nixon did it to the tune of ten percent more dollars in 1971. Presidents George W. Bush and Barack Obama have engaged in this massive supply increase of dollars on a scale hardly imaginable a decade ago. It is no exaggeration to say that the money supply of dollars has been literally increased by in excess of 300 percent in the last three to four years alone.

This supply has dramatically impacted the value and purchasing power of the dollar as is evidenced by the dropping value of the dollar against gold in a similar time frame. In the first ten years of the new millennium, the dollar has fallen from $276.50 to $1,320 so far for 2010. This represents a 377 percent drop in the dollar's constant value against gold. Since the dollar no longer has any actual intrinsic value, it depreciates significantly when the supplies of it are substantially increased.

Confidence is the other factor that lends the dollar its value. Since the value of the greenback is ultimately based on the full faith and credit of the U.S. government, its perceived value has become of paramount importance. Confidence is a funny, transient thing that takes years, even decades to build up. It can be destroyed in days, weeks, and months.

The Al Qaida terrorists' declaration of war against the United States with 9/11 represented a blow to the confidence in the nation and its currency. The financial crisis which originated in and centered on bad U.S. investment practices has been another, psychologically more devastating one. These last few years' massive increase in government debt to an unsustainable level of $14 trillion represents still a third. As confidence in the Untied States has eroded over the last ten years, so has the perceived value of the dollar fallen commiserate with it.

You can expect the roller coaster ride of the U.S. dollar's value to continue in the future. Until and unless it is once again tied to something of real intrinsic value like gold, its fortunes will fluctuate up and more likely down based on supply, demand, and confidence. Strap on your seat-belts, it is going to be a bumpy ride.

2.7 Plastic Wealth – Being in Debt Forever Based on an Illusion

You have always been told that real wealth is based on assets, such as a house. In fact, your house is typically called the largest single investment that you will ever make. The problem with this concept is an ongoing confusion between assets and liabilities. Real wealth is not built on debt, but on assets.

Assets are actually economic resources. They can be any item that a business or individual is able to both own and control in order to create value and positive cash flow, or income. Another way of putting the concept of assets is ownership of some item of value that can be changed into cash and produces cash flow. Assets either produce cash flow now or in the future.

Liabilities, on the other hand, represent present or future demands on a business or person that have to be repaid. They create negative cash flow, or take money away from the entity or individual. Anything that takes money out of your pocket is a liability and not an asset.

Because of the fact that only items that bring money into your account actually represent wealth, many of the items that you think of as wealth are not truly representations of wealth, but are liabilities and debt. The house is only the largest example of this truth.

The entire U.S. economy and most of American society is built on this idea of debt spending creating wealth. This belief is not reality. Deficit and debt spending created wealth is not real. More dangerous than this is the fact that such spending is not sustainable.

You probably already know that most Americans and the Federal government itself both spend a great deal more than they actually earn. The government does this every time it makes a budget that exceeds the literal tax base and receipts. Consumers do this with credit cards and loans made against the value of their house. For every dollar earned, a dollar and five cents is spent. This means that our country borrows as part of every day operations in order to pay for the daily spending habits.

Such borrowing to spend has been encouraged by the government every time the economy took a dip. The Fed lowers interest rates to encourage you to borrow and spend. They intend for you to do this by making credit easy. This allows you to purchase and build up items and assets that are not based on wealth but on debt.

It has reached the point that it is no longer sustainable, as the financial crisis and Great Recession have made clear. National growth has been necessary just to keep the country and consumers ahead of the rising interest and debt levels. The built up effect of such unending growth, accompanying lending, and charging of interest have pushed the increase of the money supply so that there is enough money to repay the interest due.

It has been going on at an increasingly greater level since the 1930's. This compounding effect of constantly requiring more and more money has grown like a snowball rolling down a hill. It has reached the point that it is ready to crash off of the cliff and to destroy everything in its path.

You should remember that real wealth is built on tangible assets that produce positive cash flow. Debt spending to purchase such assets does not qualify as legitimate wealth. The next time that someone holds up his or her house as an evidence of their wealth, inquire how much their monthly payments on it are. If the house is taking money out of their pockets, then it is not real wealth, but a liability, which is a fake and unsustainable wealth.

Chapter 3

The Time Is Right for Precious Metal Investment Profit

"The two most important requirements for major success are: first, being in the right place at the right time, and second, doing something about it."—Ray Kroc

Some pundits will tell you that the gold and silver markets have already run a long way up. As you will see in this chapter, there are a variety of reasons for why the timing and argument for entering gold and silver investments has seldom been better than it is these days.

3.1 Silver Is the New Gold

Among the many arguments in favor of gold and silver are the facts that they have intrinsic value. As you saw in the last chapter, intrinsic value is a tangible value inherent in an item. Intrinsic values are not simply those that an item may possess for a certain amount of time, even if that time is a long span of time. Intrinsic values are those that are good forever. This refers to an item whose value is as constant today as it proved to be thousands of years ago, over all of those long millenniums.

Very few items actually possess intrinsic value like gold and silver, except shelter and food. This is because these precious metals have remained in heavy demand for all of these thousands of years. Their other characteristic that gives them real intrinsic value is the fact that they are still capable of buying the same amount of goods now as they did even in the ancient world.

An example of this that is always given out is an expensive custom suit. A hundred years ago, such a suit could be purchased for a $20 gold piece comprised of one ounce of gold. Today the same suit will cost you about $1,200, which is actually less than a single ounce of gold.

What other asset in the world can make the same claim as gold and silver?

Intrinsic value can also be described as the item's real value or actual usefulness. Gold is useful for making beautiful jewelry and as a historic store of value, much as it has been for at least five thousand years. Silver on the other hand, has tremendous usefulness as a component of its value. You may have heard that silver has ten thousand different uses in the modern day manufacturing process. There is not any other material on earth, besides maybe oil, that has so many practical applications.

Diversity proves to be a key component of silver's amazing intrinsic value. Silver is used in most any item that is a part or process of you normal day. The one of a kind metal possesses strength, beauty, ductility, malleability, sensitivity to light, thermal and electrical conductive properties, reflective properties, and the useful capability of resisting vast changes in temperature.

All of these characteristics permit scientists and engineers alike to utilize silver for revolutionary research that meaningfully impacts your quality of life. This demand for the metal silver finds its basis in three principal pillars, those of industrial and decorative applications, photography needs, and silverware and jewelry. Between the three of them, in excess of 95 percent of the silver utilized every year is consumed. It is also interesting for you to know how much more silver goes into industrial applications than goes into jewelry. Almost three times as much silver is used every year for industrial uses as is used for jewelry needs.

Silver is in intensely heavy demand for industrial sectors ranging from electronics, to imaging, to coinage, to jewelry, to water purification, to superconductivity. Silver makes superior batteries, which are increasingly finding their way as the replacement to lithium ion batteries in both laptops and cell phones. It is an important component of heavy bearings that are used in trucks and jet engines.

It makes superior brazing and soldering materials for joining other metals together at high temperatures. Silver is also a major catalyst in industrial change processes. Finally, silver's industrial uses encompass a wide range of electronics of which it is a critical component, such as switches, television screens, and circuit boards. There is no overstating the useful component of the intrinsic value of silver.

Because of gold and silver's highly enduring intrinsic value, they can both be exchanged for goods with reliable certainty. This is as true today as it was in the Ancient Greek and Roman worlds, in the medieval towns and kingdoms of Europe, or in the modern age in any corner of the world.

As sad as it is to ponder, you can not say with any confidence whether you will be able to use a paper currency such as the dollar for a reliable quantity of goods and services fifty years from now. You can count on gold and silver being effective stores of value that will purchase a comparable or greater amount of goods and services in the future as they do now.

Gold and silver are more popular as real money now than they have been since the gold standard was abandoned in 1971. There is a site called GoldMoney.com that allows individuals to set up accounts based in gold. The money in these accounts can then be used to purchase any goods and services available over the Internet. Some states like Montana have even gone so far as to make gold a legal tender currency for use in commercial transactions within the state.

These are just two more example of how these two precious metals can be used in the exchange for goods with unfailing confidence. As world governments continue to debase and over print their paper currencies, you can count on seeing a greater number of people turn back to gold as the ultimate store of value and even currency with which to purchase goods and services. This is because unlike any paper currency, be it the dollar, euro, or pound, gold and silver have real intrinsic value whose worth is not based on simply a faith in or the credit of any government or organization.

3.2 Silver Works in the Real World

Something else that gold and silver can successfully claim over paper money is a far longer track record and history of actual utilization. Paper money finds its origins a few hundred years ago in the early modern age in Europe as a promise to pay gold. The Chinese used it in the seventh century in their empire, but with the caveat that it could be changed in for metal money at any time. Gold and silver were used as mediums of exchange long before today's concept of money even existed.

Gold first found its way into jewelry by 3000 BC. The Sumerian Royal Tombs in Ur contained such gold jewelry and art, in what is now Southern Iraq. By 1500 BC, gold had evolved to become the standard basis of inter kingdom and regional trade in the Middle East. Even as far away as South America, the Chavin civilization found uses for gold in ornaments and trade by 1200 BC.

The first gold and silver coins actually proved to be a combination of the two precious metals called electrum. The ancient Kingdom of Lydia located in Turkey holds the honor of being the first place to manufacture such coins. They did this about 650 BC with their coins that had a Lion head on them.

About a hundred years later, the Lydians developed an advanced process of separating out silver and gold into the two metal elements. They introduced these first gold coins by 560 BC. It took only two hundred years for individual gold coins and silver coins to develop into the world's currency standard that became utilized in all forms of trade. This resulted from the Persian Empire capturing the Lydian capital Sardis only thirteen years after they such gold coins had first been created. The Persian Emperor Cyrus stared in amazement at the gold coins that he found in the Kingdom of Lydia and determined that he would produce such coins himself.

With the Persians discovering how to mint gold coins, they spread their use of them all over their empire that spanned from India in the East to Libya and Egypt in the Southwest and Northern Greece and Thrace in the Northwest.

Silver also has a long and distinguished history. Mankind has been aware of it and using it since Prehistoric times. Its discovery occurred just after that of copper and gold. The Bible references it for the first time in history in Genesis. Silver was considered to be the second most perfect metal after gold. The ancients regarded silver as a practically sacred metal assuring that it would be utilized for special purposes such as coinage.

Silver coins gained great popularity as a currency in the city states of Ancient Greece. While the Persians were spreading the use of gold coins throughout the East and Middle East, the Greeks traded far and wide throughout the entire Mediterranean using their beloved silver coins. Their colonies found as far away as Southern Spain used silver coins in daily trade and transactions.

Between the efforts of the Persians and the Greeks, gold and silver coinage developed into the world standards for money that was accepted all over the known world. This did not change with time. Gold and silver coins have proven to be the only enduring standard of money all the way up to your own day and time.

Until only forty years ago, gold and silver were still the basis of even paper money. As mentioned before, paper money traces its history back to the Chinese who first invented paper in the second century AD. They had invented and began using paper money that they called flying money in the seventh century. Their paper money included the promise that it could be converted into real money coins at any point.

Thus, the first paper money, and most paper money that followed if for many centuries, only represented the actual money of gold and silver. This made it a promissory note of sorts, a promise by a government to exchange it for real money based on gold or silver.

The concept of paper money as a substitute for real gold and silver money did not gain acceptance in Europe for a long time afterward. Marco Polo returned from his epic adventures to China attempting to explain to his countrymen that in the East they used paper money to represent actual metal money. He was laughed at by his fellow Europeans.

Paper money arose in the sixteen hundreds in Europe. The Bank of England printed some of the first widely accepted of these Goldsmith notes. They, like the ancient Chinese paper notes, represented promissory notes to pay gold for deposits on account. The notes contained a promise to pay the note bearer on demand for so many pounds in gold. Once again, the paper did not turn out to be the money. The gold that underlay the paper promises proved to be the money.

Subsequent efforts at creating widely accepted paper money continued as Central Banks began to arise and take over the functions of issuing currency in the modern world. In the United States and Great Britain, this happened in the 1700's and 1800's. Standardized paper money proved to be popular and enduring. Yet it still only represented a promise to pay the holder a set amount of gold or in some cases silver. These silver certificates are highly sought out by collectors today.

An experiment with true paper money that did not represent actual gold or silver money began only forty years ago. The jury is still out on how long such paper currency backed up by only government promises will endure. One thing is for certain, it will be a long time before stand alone paper money has a significant track record behind it like gold and silver currency, and the hybrid notes that merely represented it.

3.3 Gold and Silver Have a Long History Together

An overall boom in commodities began back in 2000 and is still very much ongoing. Some have questioned how much longer this ten year long commodity run can continue to last, since the gains have been so spectacular already. Gold is up from $272 in 2000 to over $1,340 so far in 2010.

This represents an impressive over 390 percent gain so far, averaging over 30 percent returns per year. Silver is similarly performing well. Having begun the decade at an average of $5 per ounce, it has gained to about $23 per ounce so far in 2010. This also represents a major gain of three hundred and 65 percent, translating to more than 30 percent average gains per year for ten years.

In light of these astonishing gains in the two precious metals, it is understandable that you may be in the ranks of those who are afraid of getting on to the gold and silver metals train after it has finished its monumental run. This happening now is unlikely to be the case for a variety of reasons.

The first reason for this is that bull markets typically run for twenty year time periods. If you were to take a look back at the history of such commodity bull markets, then you would find that none of them lasted for less than fifteen to sixteen years. In fact, the average commodity bull market runs closer to twenty years. This is just the nature of the commodities cycle.

The twenty years before the major run began in 2000 mostly represented a twenty year bear market cycle. When you consider the sixteen to twenty year period that commodity bull runs always last, then you can relax in knowing that we are only ten years into this particular commodity bull run.

The next reason that you should not be afraid that the commodity bull market will continue is because of the underlying supply and demand fundamentals for both silver and gold. The demand for both has been rising in the wake of the Great Recession, while supply is at a stand still or in decline.

Gold is the first case study of this. Even at record high prices, gold continues to be in high demand from India and China. The people of these two countries mostly buy it in the form of gold jewelry and are expected to continue to do so. Retail investment from Europe and the United States continues to grow and reduce available gold supplies.

In the last few years, the U.S. mint has even had to suspend orders for gold coins for the year on several different occasions as they ran out of bullion blanks to utilize. Besides this, gold demand in China is anticipated to expand significantly over a longer term time frame. Not only is the Chinese Central Bank looking to increase its percentage of reserves that are kept in gold whenever it can, but The People's Bank of China has recently produced a report that they expect will encourage the demand for private individual gold for investments in the near future.

Also, demand for gold in some electronics has picked up with the expanding global recovery. All of these demand factors point to an increase in the need for gold at a time when supplies simply are tight.

Gold supplies mined from the ground are no longer growing as they once were. This is despite the fact that with record high prices, companies that are able to produce gold are aggressively trying to mine and sell more of it from remote parts of the world. In fact, the worldwide gold production is actually in a terminal decline in spite of these ever expanding highs for gold. Aaron Regent, the president of the world's largest gold mining company Barrick Gold, has said that the worldwide production of gold has actually been declining by about a million ounces of gold per year since the beginning of the gold bull market run back in 2000.

To make matter worse, the total gold mine supply has actually plummeted by ten percent with ore quality dissipating. Regent claims that Peak Gold may have already been reached. This is the point where the future output of gold will only decline year on year going forward, as all of the easily mined gold has already been extracted from the earth.

Since production peaked in 2000 and has steadily declined since that point, and Barrick Gold predicts that the decline will only continue and intensify as gold ore is becoming harder to find, the supplies of gold will only continue to tighten over time. This fundamental, coupled with the steady and rising demand, should continue to support the gold bullion bull market for years to come.

Silver's story is the same as gold's where demand is concerned. The demand for silver has been outstripping supply since 1996 or earlier. The demand only continues to grow for silver as its industrial uses are expanded with new applications found for the versatile metal with practically every passing day.

Some experts have claimed that the yearly shortfall in silver could increase to up to two hundred and fifty million ounces of silver as new demands for silver grow and expand in popularity. This sounds far more significant when you consider that the present above ground inventories for silver are only six hundred million ounces.

The growing demand for silver is what will ultimately support the prices and even take them significantly higher. When silver reached its previous peak in 1980 at about $42.50 per ounce, fully one and a half billion additional ounces of silver billion existed than do now. Yet the price still shot up to nearly $50 an ounce.

Demand for silver is what will drive it once again. The difference between 1980 and now is that a shift has taken place in the amount of silver that is available, all the while the many industrial uses and investment demands for silver are steadily and surely increasing.

Between the historical facts of bull market minimum fifteen year cycles and the rising demand and falling supplies for silver and gold, the needed fundamentals to keep the price steady and rising are present. All that you have to do is to take a look at the numbers. You will overcome your fears of having missed out on the bull market in silver and gold when you do.

3.4 The Limitations of Gold

Besides commodities inherent supply and demand imbalances that are only growing and worsening with time, there are other strong reasons to own gold and silver now. One of the chief of these is as a hedge against currency inflation. Currency inflation is something that you have been hearing a lot about in the news these days, and as the Federal Reserve prepares to engage in yet another round of quantitative easing, you have certainly not heard the last of the discussion about the imminent inflation that will come back to haunt you and all Americans one day soon.

Quantitative easing is easy to explain. It is the process whereby the government creates magic money literally out of thin air and then injects it into the economy in a desperate attempt to jump start the heart of the economic patient that is still very much on life support.

The downside to this practice is that as the money supply is expanded dramatically, and the numbers of goods and services that these dollars chase remain flat or only increase a little at the same time, then the cost of the goods and services will be pushed up as a direct result, perhaps even significantly. This is called inflation, and in cases where too much money printing and quantitative easing goes on, it can get out of hand and lead to hyperinflation.

Inflation is always a currency driven event, and you can not protect your money from inflation by simply keeping it in that currency and hoping for the best. The reason that this proves to be the case is because the purchasing power of the money that you have goes into a full blown decline as the prices of the things that you need, like food, clothes, medicines, and shelter, all rise.

In order to protect yourself and your money from the imminent and insidious threat of inflation, you have to find a vehicle to park it in that will at least keep pace with inflation, if not outperform it. You might attempt to do this with stocks, bonds, or real estate, but their effectiveness for these purposes is not assured.

The prices of all of these investments are influenced by many other factors, meaning that they might actually decline in an inflationary environment. In fact, stocks and bonds have commonly actually gone down when inflation rose significantly.

In marked contrast, gold and silver always go up in inflationary periods and environments. This is because commodities in general are positively related to inflation. Another way of putting this is that the prices of commodities tend to rise along with increasing inflation and to drop with decreasing inflation.

Recent examples of this abound. In the 1980's and 1990's, the country experienced a consistent number of years of continuously lower inflation. During these decades in general, commodity prices saw a continued and steady decline. Gold and silver also decreased in value in this period.

Today, the prices of commodities are all rising in the middle of increasing inflation. This means that as the cost of soybeans, corn, wheat, milk, and eggs go up, then you can anticipate having to pay higher amounts at the checkout line and cash register for your end food needs.

This rising inflation will certainly undermine the purchasing power of your dollars, decreasing the value of your overall wealth, if you do not do something about it. For example, if the government were to increase the money supply by ten percent, then you could expect your dollars to buy a ten percent fewer quantity of goods eventually. This means that if your hundred dollars bought thirty gallons of milk before the inflation set in, then it would buy only twenty-seven gallons afterward.

Gold and silver are famed for their properties as hedges against rising inflation. In fact, the most dependable factor that has determined the actual price of gold in the last century has proven to be inflation. As inflation rose in the past, the price of gold similarly advanced alongside it.

Following the Second World War, there have been five years in which you saw American inflation reach its highest points. These were 1946, 1974, 1975, 1979, and 1980. Consider those five telling years for a moment. In those years, the average actual return on investment in stocks, as per the Dow Jones, proved to be worse than minus 12 percent. At the same time, the average annual actual return on investments in gold turned out to be more than one hundred and 30 percent.

These days, you see a great quantity of different factors working together to lead to the possibly worst imaginable inflationary period. Between the overly accommodating monetary policy being practiced in Washington D.C. that has increased the money supply by more than 300 percent, the long term ongoing dollar decline, rises in oil prices, an increasing and astronomical trade deficit, and the United States' only rising status as the planet's largest in debt nation, inflation is a specter looking to rise up and overwhelm you if you simply sit idly by on the side lines. In most every category of commodities, the prices are rising. This has been the case lately even when the dollar strengthened temporarily, an unusual and unnatural phenomenon for commodities prices.

So many respected economists are telling you that inflation is in the economic cards. You sense it yourself every time that you hear the government talking about printing still more money to get things going again and to put the unemployed people back to work. You may be wondering what you can do to protect yourself from it.

Investing a part of your money in tangible, real, historically valued assets like gold and silver is the natural antidote to the poison of inflation. It will allow you to counter the negative inflationary pressures. As hedges against rising inflation, both gold and silver perform admirably in any country and any time period. This makes today the best time to take a position in gold and silver, before they move up any higher, and similarly before your dollars decline any further in purchasing power in the meantime.

3.5 Gold and Silver Provide the Best Defense

Yet another reason to own gold and silver today is because of the two precious metals' roles as safe havens in times of economic crises. There are two different aspects to this argument for owning gold and silver. The first is as a safe haven against a declining dollar. The second is as a safe haven against instability and crises in the world in general. Both are viable reasons underpinning the ongoing prices of gold and silver.

Gold and silver make the ultimate hedges against declining dollars for a very simple reason. Both metals are actually priced in U.S. dollars, meaning that they are both bought and sold in them. Any type of decline in the underlying dollar value means that the actual prices of gold and silver can be counted on to rise, even if not in a perfect ratio.

You might ask why this should matter. After all, the U.S. dollar still proves to be the reserve currency of the whole world. It is the basic exchange medium used in international kinds of transactions, the base currency that all equities and commodities are figured up in, the world's main place to park savings no matter what country a person lives in, and still the currency that is more held by the central banks of the world than any other rival currency.

The truth is that nothing backs it up since the abandoning of the gold standard but confidence in the full faith and credit of the U.S. government. As you have read before, confidence is a shaky thing, particularly in the day and age in which you live. It can crumple overnight, spurred on by a refusal of the Chinese to buy any more of our mountains of debt issued, or a severe terrorist attack. When the confidence goes, the value of the dollar can wilt away faster than you might believe to be possible. In the end, the dollar represents nothing more than a promise and a sophisticated piece of paper.

Gold and silver are also useful to have as safe havens in troubled times and crises. It may be true that the United States remains the only superpower in the world, but this does not change the fact that a great number of difficulties and challenges are lying in wait all over the planet.

Any of these situations could blow up with little to no warning. Gold is commonly referred to as the ultimate crisis commodity as it most always offers superior returns to other types of investments when there are times of great tension throughout the world. This is because those identical causes that lead other forms of investments to do poorly will simultaneously make the cost of gold go up.

As a case in point, poor economies can destroy banks that are badly run. Banks that go down can cause a whole economy to fall apart. On top of this, today's global economy is so tightly integrated that a single country's banking problems that lead to economic failures can shake or even bring down the economy of the entire world. These problems, such as banking crises, also cause the public to lose confidence in paper assets and currencies. When they do this, the place that they look to for a real and reliable safe haven is gold.

As crises like this develop, governments have a bad habit of turning back to their electronic printing presses. By bailing out banks and sinking economies, they only debase the existing currency more. While this is happening, gold is only gaining apace. There can be no doubt that the price of gold always goes up most significantly as confidence in the government proves to be at its lowest point.

Buying gold or silver as a safe haven will do more than simply protect your dollars and wealth from potential disaster. It will give you peace of mind that you have taken a proactive step to be prepared. In acquiring them, you can be sure that you will survive more than potential inflation. You can rest assured that you and your estate will be ready if the wheels come off of the proverbial geopolitical or global economic cart.

Chapter 4

The Story of Silver and Why It Is a Better Choice Than Gold

"You have to know the past to understand the present."—Dr. Carl Sagan

It may come as a surprise to you to learn that silver is a better investment choice than gold is right now. There are a number of reasons why this proves to be the case, and not simply one argument. This chapter goes through the eight reasons why you should acquire silver over gold for your portfolio today.

4.1 Silver Is More Than Precious

The statement that silver is rarer than gold right now is true from a particular and important point of view. When you take into account the above ground silverware and jewelry available supplies, then the grey metal is not rarer than the yellow metal proves to be. But, if you are looking at just the quantity of identifiable actually available silver bullion, then silver truly is rarer than is gold. It is an important starting point to understand that practically speaking, silver turns out to be rarer than gold.

Although silver jewelry and silverware could in theory be melted down to secure greater sources of silver, this is not likely to happen for an important reason. Gold metal jewelry trades at a tiny premium over the present market prices for the yellow metal. This means that with relatively small change in the price of gold, people could be easily persuaded to melt down their gold jewelry.

As gold has risen aggressively in the past several years, you have already started to see this happen with the rise of the many cash for your scrap gold operations that have been successfully advertising for and attracting clients to sell them their old, unwanted gold jewelry. Silver jewelry on the other hand sells at a much higher premium to its underlying precious metal value. This means that most people would not be persuaded to sell their scrap silver jewelry until prices increased by another $50-$60 more per ounce.

Strictly by the numbers though, the World Gold Council and comparable experts claim that there are somewhere between four and five billion ounces of physical gold still left in the world. This phrase "still left" is actually meaningless, since gold experts routinely point out that 95 percent of all of the actual gold that has ever been uncovered since world history began is still in existence. The truth about gold is that it is rarely consumed, or burned up. In general, it does not simply go away, but it stays with us, preserved in some form.

There was a time when this proved to be the story for silver as well. The facts on the ground regarding silver and its availability and utility have changed in an incredible fashion since the end of the Second World War. How this translates into available silver is surprising.

As you saw in the last chapter, a mere six hundred and seventy-one million ounces of silver bullion that is available for use are still found above ground, per the World Silver Survey of 2004. The updated numbers on this show that silver has been drawn down still significantly further, to a mere twenty million ounce by the end of 2009.

There literally is not much silver to go around anymore. The present supply of mined, refined, available silver bullion in the world is generally held in the warehouse of the COMEX, or the Futures and Commodities Exchange. This warehouse proves to be the greatest silver supply and inventory on the whole planet. Here are found in excess of one hundred and twenty million ounces.

This sounds like a large amount of silver, until you consider that Warren Buffet bought more silver bullion than this back in the late 1990's. Another telling sign about the tight supplies of silver situation is found in the U.S. government vaults. It was not so long ago that they maintained an inventory of a few billion ounces of available silver in the vaults for U.S. Mint coining operations and needs.

These days, it does not have inventory left to speak of at all. It is rather comical to think that eight years ago, the government had no choice but to begin buying significant quantities of silver in the world markets to be capable of continuing to mint its beloved one ounce Silver Eagle coins.

The main reason why silver is rarer than gold revolves around the demand for it. While a greater amount of gold is mined each day than is typically demanded, it is mostly preserved. This is not the case for silver. All of the silver mined each year is utilized and then some beyond that, as you saw in the last chapter.

Between industry, photography, silverware, jewelry, and coins, there simply is no longer enough silver to go around each year. This deficit for silver is nothing new. The metal has been in a real supply and demand deficit now for sixty-three years, going all the way back to 1942.

Remember as you read through the rest of this chapter the important point that the available amount of silver is now rarer than the available amount of gold. Not only are the available stocks rarer for silver than for gold, but the amount of silver mined relative to the silver demand every year causes it to have a net decline in above ground stocks each year as well.

These are some very compelling reasons for why you should consider silver as a superior opportunity to gold right now.

4.2 Silver Is on the Bargain Table

Silver has come to be more and more expensive to find and mine as it gets rarer. As silver companies have to go farther and farther afield and dig deeper to locate the dwindling supplies of it, the prices of extracting it from the ground continue to rise.

There are now silver companies that can no longer afford to bring it out of the ground practically and viably even at today's relatively higher prices of $23 per ounce. Some of them are choosing to shut down production and lay off workers as a result of how low silver prices remain when adjusted for inflation.

If silver is less highly priced than the cost of digging it out of the ground, then you could literally say that silver is cheaper than dirt.

This phrase is becoming the mantra for some silver investors. Its sentiments have been echoed by legendary commodities investor Jim Rogers, who has been recommending silver over gold since the summer of 2010. Jim made his billions as the partner of foreign currency investor George Soros when they took heavy positions against the Bank of England in the 1990s and literally made a billion dollars in a single day as their positions proved to be right on the money.

Although the billionaire Jim Rogers has been recommending gold for years and telling people that he never sells gold, but that he only buys and hold its, he has recently changed his long standing tune. Jim has announced that he is no longer buying gold, although he loves it and still believes that one day soon, everyone will own gold and will walk down the street checking the prices of it in storefront windows. Instead, he is sinking his smart money and that of his investors heavily into silver.

Jim says that the reasons for this are abundant. Silver is still at less than 50 percent of its all time high made back in 1980. Gold on the other hand is trading at all time highs seemingly all of the time lately. Jim said that silver is depressed and ridiculously cheap at these levels. When silver companies can no longer afford to mine and refine it at the world prices that are offered for it, you can expect it to appreciate higher in the near future.

4.3 Silver Is Used and Abused

You should have a good understanding of the many applications of silver. This is necessary to effective grasp the fact that more than 90 percent of annual silver production is actually burned up in being utilized in consumer goods. When these consumer goods are discarded, the silver found in them goes with them to the land fill.

Silver finds its way into ten thousand different products, a mentioned in the last chapter. There are such a wide array of silver uses that it is almost overwhelming. The fact that more than 90 percent of silver mined goes into these disposable products is a major factor behind why silver is a better investment now than gold.

As of three years ago, 455.5 million ounces of annually mined silver found their way into industrial use applications. Besides this, in excess of 128 million silver ounces went to the photography sector. Jewelry uses consumed 163.5 million ounces of silver as well. Finally, silverware represented nearly 59 million ounces of mined silver for the year.

Industrial applications for silver are so very many. Silver is used in dentistry to make amalgams that are heavily utilized in dental fillings. Here, it is combined with tin, mercury, and various other metals as a powdered form to create a stiff paste. This silver alloy dental amalgam reaches first stage of hardness in only minutes.

Silver is indispensable in mirrors and optics too. The reflective characteristic of mirrors actually comes from the silvering process, where the silver is applied as the reflective material. Silver is utilized in optics in the sputtering process, where it is put on to glass at different levels of thickness. For solar reflectors whose use is only growing each and every year, silver is always the best choice for reflective coatings.

You saw last chapter that silver is used in a variety of hardcore industrial applications, such as for batteries, catalysts, brazing and soldering, and bearings. Because of its unique properties like the ability to resist extreme changes in temperatures, it cannot simply be easily substituted out by another metal or material.

For example, silver is likely the only catalyst that can be found to change ethylene into ethylene oxide, which is useful in creating polyesters. It is also the best catalyst for oxidation reactions that are used to create methanol and formaldehyde. Silver is also frequently utilized in manufacturing control rods for pressurized water based nuclear reactors. These manufacturing industrial applications for silver are only growing with time.

Silver is useful in medicinal applications as well. As it reacts effectively with viruses, algae, bacteria, and fungus but does not poison people or make them sick, it is finding increasing uses as a germicide. Silver has found its way into the commonplace use in bandages and topical gels because of these antimicrobial properties. It is found in silver sulfadiazine cream that is used along with silver coated dressings to treat burn victims. When used in silver nanorods, silver electrodes are even more effective in killing bacteria.

Silver also is helpful in hospital and medicine applications. It is often utilized in catheters, making it indispensable in hospital applications. Its antibacterial properties help to keep down infection. Because of this, it is the choice of use as a silver alloy in various catheters. Silver is also employed in compounds that are used to manufacture colloidal silver suspensions and homeopathic solutions.

Silver is even used in clothing manufacturing today. This is again because of its unique properties for lowering the bacterial count and keeping down odors. By integrating silver nanoparticles into the polymers from which clothing is made, or by instead coating yarns using silver, it keeps socks and other clothes free of bacteria and smelling fresh.

Instrument players will also find that silver is employed in the construction of most any quality musical wind instrument. Flutes especially are built using silver alloy. The frictional properties of the metal make it especially useful for instruments.

Although the use of silver in the development of photographs has diminished considerably with the replacement of regular pictures by digital ones, silver is still increasingly used in x-ray pictures and silver halide films. These types of pictures are more accurate when they incorporate silver. Movie film companies also prefer silver halide film to digital film because of its accurate color, great resolution, and low cost.

In electronics, silver touches every aspect of your life. It is useful in coating DVDs, CDs, and plasma television panels. It finds a place in computers and cell phones. Circuit boards also would not be effectively manufactured without the use of silver, meaning that most every electronic good incorporates the use of silver.

In practically all applications that have been mentioned above, the products are discarded when their useful life expectancy has finished. The silver then goes along for the ride to the area garbage dump, where it is lost to practical use. There is no practical technology existing for recycling the silver out of these many electronic and industrial use products at anywhere near the current prices of just over $23 per ounce.

4.4 Silver Is the Happy Child of an Essential Industry

Part of the reason that silver is so hard to come by results from the way that it is found, mined, separated, and refined from its naturally occurring state. There are silver ore veins found occurring in relatively pure form that are mined. In a perfect world, this would represent the source from which most usable silver came from, but it does not in truth.

A great amount of silver has to be refined from other metals with which it is found. These include gold, with which it is commonly mixed. The combined ores of gold and silver are known as electrum.

In fact, the main sources of silver are not strictly from silver mines at all. Silver also commonly comes from ores that contain metals besides gold. The main sources of silver in the world are ores that include copper, copper and nickel, lead and zinc, and lead. Silver is mostly found in the mines of a handful of countries.

These countries are comprised of Peru, Mexico, Australia, China, Chile, Serbia, and Poland. Peru and Mexico remain the world's top silver producers, an impressive fact since they have both been producing silver since the middle of the sixteenth century. The greatest mines that produce silver are the Proaño / Fresnillo Mines of Mexico, the Dukat Mine of Russia, the Cannington Mine of Queensland, Australia, the Greens Creek Mine of Alaska, and the Uchucchacua Mine of Peru.

When silver is found mixed with other metals, as it is in most of its natural occurrences, it has to be refined and separated out in a time consuming process. Silver is in fact mostly produced as a result of the electrolytic copper refining process. It is also obtained using nickel, gold, and zinc refining. When silver is mixed with lead, the Parkes process is utilized to separate out the silver from the lead.

The electrolytic copper refining process is an involved one. In this manufacturing process, electrolysis is performed with the use of a direct electric current. An electrolytic cell is also used as part of the procedure. This cell works with the electrical energy inputted in order to decompose and break down the chemical compounds. This creates a specific chemical reaction that helps to separate out the silver and the copper. Such electrolysis is necessary commercially to separate out the silver from its copper ores.

Refining silver out from nickel, gold, and zinc is also an involved and time consuming process. In such refining, the metals are superheated in a melted form. Once they are turned into this molten metal form, they can then be oxidized or poured off.

The Parkes process is similarly used to produce silver bullion from lead. It actually involves extracting the metals in a liquid from liquid process. It works because silver proves to be fully three hundred times more dissolvable in zinc than it actually is in lead. The process works effectively when zinc is poured in to lead that is has been liquefied and contains silver inside of it.

In the process, the silver is attracted to the zinc over the lead. Zinc is far more easily removed form the silver then, since it remains within its own layer. The two are heated, the zinc migrates to its own layer, and pure silver remains behind. Gold can also be taken out of lead in utilizing this Parkes process.

Silver that is suitable for commercial uses has to be refined to a high level of purity. This means that silver must reach a minimum of 99.9 percent purity to be suitable for all of its many applications in the world. Some applications require it to be 99.99 percent pure. This also requires super heating the metal to separate out the impurities found within the metal. As the silver becomes molten, the impurities rise to the surface and can be poured off.

Now you begin to understand why it is so difficult to produce silver on a great scale that is necessary to keep up with the constantly rising industrial, jewelry, photographic, silver ware, and coin applications and demand. This intensive process of actually getting silver to the point from a mixed up ore form to the purified product that it is useful helps to explain the relatively high cost of producing a single ounce of the grey metal. It also goes to show you a main reason why it is so hard to find new silver mines in the world today, since silver is so commonly mixed in with other metals.

4.5 Silver Production Is Low

When you look back on silver production and inventories since World War II, a shocking picture emerges. Consider this, at the end of the Second World War, the world's entire known supplies of silver totaled up to fully ten billion ounces. Four billion ounces of this total, representing a 40 percent holding, were in the hands of the U.S. government and its vaults.

Back then, an age of unparalleled growth in the world economy began. It lasted more or less until the Great Recession of 2007. During these years, silver began to be used up in a wide range of essential modern day applications. This happened at an increasing and fantastic rate.

Ten years ago, the world silver above ground available stocks were down to a still significant 500 million ounces. Two years ago, they were down to 144 million ounces existing. The end of 2009 saw these supplies drop more than 120 million ounces to 20 million ounces total, a staggering drop that indicates a problem with supply.

What could have caused this staggering drop in supplies? Is silver production down so far from the end of World War II? In fact it has dropped most years until just a few years ago. Silver production has stabilized in the last few years and is even up a little bit over a year on year timeframe. This still is not sufficient to arrest the net supply and demand imbalance.

And when you look at silver supplies from the year 2000 until 2009, they are still down over the ten year period. Once again, this is despite rising silver prices throughout most of the decade. The price in silver has improved from less than $5 per ounce at the beginning of the millennium to more than $23 per ounce in 2010.

Yet despite all of the incentive for silver producers to mine, separate out, and refine silver this decade, the production of silver has dropped from 919 million ounces and change in the year 2000 to 889 million ounces in 2009. This represents a 3.3 percent drop in world silver production over one of the greatest periods of price increase for the metal in modern history.

One reason that the supply of available silver has declined while in the midst of the bull market for the metal lies in the fact that 75 percent of all silver production occurs as a direct result of the by product mining of copper, lead, and zinc, as discussed earlier in the chapter.

The decline in the world economy surrounding the Great Recession led to a significant reduction in the demand of these so-called base metals. As the demand for such metals as copper, lead, and zinc deteriorated, a number of mining outfits shut in production and laid off staff. Some even closed base metal mines down.

The ensuing reduction in base metal supply therefore had a dramatic impact on the available supply of silver as well. On top of this, a number of companies that mined silver as their primary product, which made up the remaining 25 percent of yearly production, chose to close down mines and operations as a result of the poor numbers surrounding silver pricing when adjusted for inflation.

Sunshine Mining is one of these that made this decision. It will take them years to ramp production back up to where it was at the beginning of the decade, if they ever manage to do so.

The imbalance between silver production and demand has proven to be astonishing in recent years. In the year 2000, silver production along with the sale of scrap silver was 772 million ounces while demand proved to be 919 million ounces.

This means that fully 147 million more ounces of silver were demanded than were produced. In 2004, this silver production plus the sale of scrap silver was 797 million ounces, while the demand proved to be 868 million ounces.

Even though the fundamentals had improved, still in excess of 71 million ounces of silver had to be drawn down from an already dwindling stockpile. In 2009, the most recent data that is available, the gap between silver production and silver demand had almost disappeared as a result of the diminished demand from the Great Recession.

The shortfall was down to only around 14 million ounces of silver. This is just in time too, since the total available world stocks of silver are now around 20 million ounces.

Silver metal is the one that has the lowest quantity of reserves to production, as well as the lowest reserve base to production ratios. Of all the metals commercially mined and utilized today, silver proves to be the one that is closest to the Hubert's Peak, or peak production.

Hubert's Peak refers to the point where there will be less of a raw material produced going forward than was in the past, because the easiest half of the resources to mine have already been brought above ground.

The silver ounces that remain in the ground will be brought up at increasingly higher costs, peak production silver argues. That will result from the silver that remains being found in more remote parts of the earth, at deeper levels that are harder to access.

You will hear more and more about peak silver as time goes along. The time to buy silver for your investment portfolio is now, before the concept of Peak Silver gets to be a household word. By buying silver in advance of this, you will gain the benefit of owning it at prices that do not at all reflect the reality of peak silver, nor the prices that will come with it once the secret gets out.

4.6 The Gold and Silver Relationship – Can I Have the Next Dance?

In the past, silver and gold have historically and generally maintained a stable and reliable relationship between their prices. Throughout most of history, this ratio has revolved around 1:12. The buying power of gold was supposed to be around twelve times that of silver in reality.

This is the way it was in much of the last five thousand years of precious metals relationship and history. Twelve ounces of silver would buy the same amount of goods or services as would one ounce of gold. For example, if silver was trading at $10 per ounce, then gold would be priced for $120 per ounce, or for twelve ounces of silver per one ounce of gold.

This revelation may have you scratching your head. When was the last time that you saw gold trading at anywhere near such a close ratio to the price of silver? Certainly not since 1980, when silver briefly reached a short term peak high of around $50 per ounce to gold's less than $800 per ounce price at the same time.

Instead, today you see a buying power, or price ratio between gold and silver, that is much closer to 1:55. In fact, in the first week of October, it actually worked out to be higher than this at in excess of 1:58. This had gold trading at over $1,350 per ounce while silver was languishing at merely just over $23 per ounce. Languishing is perhaps a harsh word for these prices of silver, since it is trading at highs not seen since the early 1980's these days.

Still, gold's recent run has been nothing short of amazing, as it has shattered its historic all time highs on multiple occasions in the last several weeks, as well as years. This begs the question, is the old ratio of 1:12 between silver and gold dead and buried, or is something more set to happen that will adjust the ratio back to the historic norms?

There are other ways of looking at this ratio and trying to figure out the numbers. One of these is the amount of available stocks of above ground silver versus above ground gold. Twenty million ounces of silver stock remain above ground.

Approximately 260 million ounces worth of gold are above ground these days. When you do the math, you actually come up with thirteen times as much above ground gold as available silver. This goes to show you how much rarer available silver proves to be today than gold is.

Even though the demand for gold for investment purposes is greater than silver's demand for the same, silver more than makes up for this with its massive industrial applications demand, as you have seen in the last chapters.

Another ratio to compare between gold and silver is the annual production of gold versus silver. Around 85 million ounces of gold were produced in 2009 to silver's 710 million ounces. This ratio amounts to nearly exactly twelve to one. So the amount of silver produced in a year is still twelve to one versus gold, on a level that is supposed to make the purchasing power of gold only twelve times higher than silver.

Looking at these important other ratios of gold to silver of above ground available stocks and annual production tells you that something is out of line with the present fifty-eight to one ratio of gold prices to silver prices. Gold is produced at a twelve to one ratio as is silver, and yet available silver is far rarer than is gold with thirteen times as much gold available as is silver. This argues for substantially higher silver prices in the future.

Consider for a minute what would happen if this historic ratio came back into alignment at today's gold prices. With gold at over $1,350 per ounce, the old 12:1 ratio between gold and silver would mean that silver prices would rise to a shocking level of $112.50. This is not as far fetched as it might at first seem to you, when you consider the inflation adjusted prices of silver at its 1980 high of around $50 per ounce.

In today's dollars, that would have silver rising to over $160 per ounce. Looked at from this historical inflation adjusted high, silver does not seem so ludicrously overpriced even at the $112.50 per ounce that it should be at based on gold's recent stratospheric numbers.

Naturally, this will not happen overnight. Silver has a long way to go left in this bull market though. How long will it take to run from $23 per ounce to $112.50 per ounce or higher is hard to say. As it represents a four hundred and 90 percent price increase from the present silver price levels, it could be several years.

Silver at $23 per ounce suddenly does not seem so high any more when you look at the historic 12:1 price ratios between gold and silver, as well as the inflation adjusted high for silver set thirty years ago. You should look into acquiring it cheaply at today's relatively low prices adjusted for inflation, while you still can.

4.7 From Grandma's Photograph to Heart Monitors

You may be wondering how the decline of traditional photography in favor of digital photography has been impacting one of the key demands for silver. This lies in the utilization of silver in making film.

As of the most recent data that the Silver Institute offered on the subject in 2007, silver used for the photography industry represented 128 million ounces of silver. This proved to be a significant 16 percent of the annual demand for silver.

Critics of silver have clapped gleefully at how this changing trend would represent the demise of the gray metal, as people shifted away from using film to develop pictures. Has it proven to be the case so far though, many years into the digital camera revolution? Just a few years before 2007, the film photography industry accounted for roughly 224 million ounces of silver.

This represented around 28 percent of the silver use for the year. By 2007, the percentage of silver demand that was taken up by photography had plummeted to only 16 percent, and yet silver demand and prices continue to rise.

Despite the fact that traditional cameras and film sales have been on the decline, the demand for silver has not fallen off as many experts gleefully predicted. Several things explain this. Even with the advent of digital cameras gradually taking over the photography business, traditional silver oxide photographic prints have not died out. This is because of a few considerations. Even reasonably good digital cameras still do not take pictures that print out in good resolution using a color inkjet printer. These printer cartridges are not cheap, despite the fact that they have been around for years. Yet, they consume ink for digital photo prints like it was abundant and free.

Besides this fact, any really important pictures are still printed out on high quality silver oxide photo paper. This includes wedding photography, special events, and first pictures of a new grandchild. X-rays are still primarily printed out on high quality silver paper too. Beyond this, in the developing world, picture taking has become a popular past time for the average citizen.

Places like China actually sell more and not less real film and photo processing services now than in the past. This keeps this category of silver use alive and well, allowing it to decline only gradually instead of sharply.

A good parallel for the supposed death of physically printed out photographs is the advent of the computer and the so called paperless office. Even though computers were supposed to spell the death of the traditional paperwork in offices, the opposite has occurred. Recycling bins full of paper at most any office are proof of this fact.

As you saw earlier in this chapter, silver reinvents itself for industrial purposes constantly. The metal finds new and more uses for itself all of the time. Many of these are in cutting edged and rapidly growing industries and in high technology and in demand products, such as in cell phones, iPods, computers, solar panels, and water treatment plant technology.

The growth in these other areas continues to outpace any declines in photography developing services and film. Such growth is projected to continue to do so in the future.

The proof for silver surviving the continuous decline of physical film and developing services is already out. Even though the percentage of silver consumed in such activities has somewhat sharply declined from 28 percent to 16 percent, silver demand continues to build and expand over time.

Rather than the prices of silver having declined along with the slowly dying industry of traditional film photography, they are instead increasing at an impressive pace. Silver will continue to be more and more indispensable to a growing number of other fields with time. This will assure that the metal continues to perform well on a demand side of the equation going forward.

4.8 Silver's Love Affair with Electrons

Silver proves to have so many amazing and sometimes irreplaceable uses as a result of its ability to conduct electricity so well. You are probably not aware of this, but silver proves to be the very best conductor of electricity known to man.

Copper may have been more commonly used in the past for wiring applications, but all of that is about to change forever. Because silver is such an amazing conductor of electricity in any temperature range, a whole new generation of wiring, called HTS wiring, that is being rolled out throughout the United States, is made with silver as its critical component.

This HTS wire effectively carries an astonishing one hundred and forty times as much current as does traditional copper wire. It is capable of this carrying capacity only because it utilizes silver because of its conductivity, strength, and flexibility.

These HTS wires are the future for the nation's electric grid. The Department of Energy plans on promoting the many applications for these silver based HTS wires through funding a nationwide program that will improve the reliability, efficiency, and capacity of the electric power system of delivery.

Transmission losses can be reduced by an impressive eight percent with these new HTS wires, helping to cut down substantially on oil imports. The government is similarly planning the installation of a ten megavolt HTS based transformer into the national electric grid. These HTS based transformers prove to be free of oil and far more environmentally friendly. HTS conductors are also significantly more efficient. Not simply useful for traditional carrying and distribution wiring though, they can be utilized in a wide range of applications, including electric motors.

The demand for electric motors is only expected to grow over time. When HTS wires become increasingly more widespread, experts say that they will be included in the full line of electronic and electrical devices that will run the spectrum from the biggest electric motors to all electronics, even including toys.

Besides this important and potentially revolutionary new use for silver, it is increasingly finding other high tech uses. Silver is essential in tagging device wireless RIFF technology. It is heavily used in hospitals, as you saw in the past chapters. There is practically no electronic device of which it is not a part, whether you are talking about toasters, refrigerators, cell phones, televisions, or CDs. The best electrical conductor will only become more important in the future and with time.

By buying silver now, you can grow with it as it comes increasingly to dominate the world in which you live. Silver's uses are only projected to escalate. Meanwhile, the supplies of it are rapidly dwindling around the world that has increasingly become one of Peak Silver.

How high silver might go as this realization sinks in is hard to predict. There are now pundits out there claiming that silver will one day sell on a par with gold, at a literal one to one ratio. Even if this fantastic prediction proves to be only partially true, the sky may not prove to be the limit for the future price appreciation of silver, the grey metal.

4.9 Silver Leasing - A Bubble Soon to Pop

Silver leasing is an interesting concept that you have possibly heard of in the past but probably do not understand. For those of you who are prepared to make a significant investment in silver, it is helpful to comprehend what silver leasing is and involves. This is because silver leasing impacts the price of silver, even to the extent of holding it down.

Silver leasing works along the same principal as does gold leasing. Neither of them are really leasing at all. Leasing is a term commonly used in real estate that refers to a property being rented in exchange for monthly rent payments. No one is renting any silver in a leasing arrangement.

First of all, most silver in the world can not be loaned out, as it is being used to meet the physical demand of industrial and commercial uses discussed in depth earlier in the book. Most owners of silver have a use for it, and will only be pressed into selling it if the price per ounce motivates them to do so.

This is not the case with those who engage in silver leasing. There are some silver owners who are more concerned with getting an interest rate locked in on their silver holdings. In this case, they do not care about the price per ounce of their silver, but only what they can get as an interest rate in the transaction of leasing it out.

But they are not leasing it out at all; they are actually selling it in exchange for a locked in interest rate. When they sell this silver, they do not receive the earnings off the transaction, but instead a fixed interest rate and a promise that the silver will be returned to them on a certain day.

The easiest form of silver leasing to understand is that done by the central banks like the Federal Reserve. In such a practice, the Fed literally takes its silver to a bullion bank. A bullion bank is a large bank institution that acts as an intermediary for silver and gold leasing. The banking majors like Citigroup, Bank of America, Barclays, JP Morgan Chase Bank, Goldman Sachs, and UBS all function as major bullion banks.

A bullion bank will commonly pay the Central Bank one percent interest on the silver that it leases from them. Along with this interest rate, the bullion banks provide the Central Bank with a guarantee to give them their silver back on a certain pre-determined future date. The Central Bank is happy because it gets paid for loaning out its silver. You are probably wondering what the bullion bank gets from the arrangement.

Bullion banks are not engaging in this leasing of silver for speculation on silver prices, as you might suppose. Rather they are only interested in obtaining the gray metal in order to sell it on the international open silver market. They then take the money that they receive from the sale and purchase a government guaranteed investment such as Treasury bonds that come with a net return of from three to four percent.

You have probably already seen the potential weakness in this arrangement on the part of the bullion banks. What do the bullion banks like JP Morgan Chase, Goldman Sachs, and Barclays do if the prices of silver rise after they have sold it and when it is time for them to buy it back and return it?

Bullion banks have thought of this danger and address it with the use of futures. In the futures market, they are able to purchase a contract on silver that allows them to fix both a delivery date and price for their needed quantities of silver. This does cost them something from their profits on the arrangement, but it removes all risk from the transaction.

Obtaining a one to two percent return after costs and having absolutely no risk on the arrangement is a fantastic deal for the bullion banks. The Central Bank who lent the silver out receives a one percent return rather than the zero return that silver resting in their vaults earns them, so they are happy with the transaction. Since this deal proves to be a winning situation for both bullion banks and central banks, who loses in the procedure?

The case has been made that individual silver investors are the ones losing on the arrangement. Critics of the whole process argue that the practice of silver leasing is literally but artificially boosting the supply of silver available for investment, commercial, and industrial needs. This keeps the real prices of the actual physical silver down, since there is always twice as much silver listed in physical inventory stocks as is involved in any leasing arrangement.

Neither bullion banks nor central banks care what the price of silver will be, since their returns are both fixed up front and assured. Because of this, silver leasing artificially distorts the actual supply and demand correlation that should exist between sellers and buyers.

There is a theory that insists that using this leasing to keep down the prices of silver and gold is not merely a side effect, but an intentional design. Alan Greenspan has made the statement that central banks are prepared to lease precious metals in greater amounts if the prices for them continue to increase. Some economists argue that if gold and silver leasing did not occur, that the paper money currencies of governments today would seem to be essentially without worth as they quickly dropped in value against both silver and gold.

This theory is supported by the fact that a known deficit in silver mined and supplied versus silver demanded has existed for a great number of years, as you saw earlier in the book. When a commodity has more being consumed than is produced, the laws of economics say that for each day, month, or year of such a deficit, it has to be balanced out by withdrawals from existing stock piles.

This has in fact been going on for years, until there are only merely 20 million ounces available in the collective stockpile, versus the five to six billion ounces that existed following the Second World War.

Because there was a deficit in silver and increasingly falling stock piles, something has to explain why the prices of silver did not respond for many years. The shortfall appeared to be offset by the silver that came to market in the form of silver leasing. This did not prove to be real silver, but only silver on paper, since the same silver could not be owned by a Central Bank and by a bullion bank at the same time. Instead it was only borrowed. Yet by accounting methods and on paper, every million ounces that the central banks loaned out showed up as two million ounces in physical supplies.

The end result of this concerns the possible end of silver leasing. If silver leasing becomes illegal, it will have a profound effect on the silver market and price. With no more false distortion in the amount of silver actually available, the extremely tight supplies on the market will finally filter through to price more rapidly and accurately. You could see silver prices galloping higher when that day eventually comes. There has been talk about the end of silver leasing as a practice for some time; if it finally happens, the immediate move higher in silver prices will be truly breathtaking.

Chapter 5

How You Can Make a Fortune Investing in Silver

"Too many people miss the silver lining

because they're expecting gold."—Maurice Setter

The silver supply and demand imbalance simply means that there is no longer enough silver to go around. The above ground stocks are almost non-existent at 20 million ounces.

With only one more deficit year production of silver versus its demand for the year, there will no longer be sufficient amounts of the gray precious metal for the existing needs.

Even though the price for silver seems high at the multi year peak of $23 per ounce (as of this writing), this is only the case when you detach the silver prices from their historical highs and ignore the inflation adjusted highs and silver to gold ratios as well.

Remember that the all time high for silver is still at near $50 per ounce. As the legendary commodities billionaire investor Jim Rogers has so astutely pointed out on more than one occasion, this represents as a 55 percent discount to the all time high that was set back in the early 1980s.

5.1 Timing, Markets, and Value – Looking Good Right Now

What would you rather invest in, gold that has surpassed its all time high several different times already, or silver that still has more than 117 percent price appreciation left before it reaches the high?

To put it in practical terms, $10,000 invested in silver at today's prices could be worth more than $21,500 if silver reclaimed its constant dollar high. For constant dollar price appreciation opportunity, there are few investments out there that offer you the opportunities that silver does right now.

You must not forget either that the $50 high price of silver only represents a constant dollar high. The actual inflation adjusted high for silver is somewhere closer to $165 per ounce, when 1980 dollars are converted into 2010 dollars. By this measurement, silver still has a long, long way to go.

According to the inflation adjusted high for silver, it is trading at an astonishing discount of 86 percent to its true value dollar high price. In other words, silver has more than a whopping 615 percent in price appreciation potential left to it before it reaches its inflation adjusted high again of from $23 per ounce to $165 dollars per ounce.

If you put $10,000 into silver at today's prices and watched it reach the inflation adjusted high, then you would have more than $61,500 in profits when all was said and done.

Using the gold to silver historic ratios of 1:12, you see that silver also has enormous price movement potential. Silver to gold is valued at 1:58 pricing ratio these days, as you read in the last chapter. But should silver realign to its traditional average of 1:12 purchasing power of gold to silver, than the silver prices would similarly be far higher.

With gold at $1,350 per ounce, silver's historical ratio price to gold would have it at $112.50 per ounce. This figure also has silver trading at a substantial discount presently of around 80 percent to its proper gold to silver ratio. Using this figure as the proper value for silver, then you have the possibility of 390 percent returns from the present levels of silver at $23 per ounce to the historical gold to silver 1:12 ratio price of $112.50.

In practical dollar terms, this means that $10,000 invested in silver at today's prices would yield a $39,000 profit if silver realigned to its traditional gold to silver pricing ratio.

There can be no doubt that the price potential appreciation is there for silver. This is true whether you look towards its all time high, inflation adjusted high, or historical gold to silver price ratio. Now that you see why you have to invest in silver today, you need to understand the various vehicles for doing this. They all have their own advantages and disadvantages, as you will read about in the rest of the chapter. But first, you will read about why there is another ten years left to the incredible silver bull market run left.

5.2 The Twenty Year Cycle and Silver

With these incredible percentage appreciation possibilities for silver presently ranging from 117 percent, to 390 percent, to 615 percent, depending on the way that you figure the fair price for silver in today's dollars, you may wonder how long a period this might take to transpire. The answer to your question has everything to do with the length of commodity cycles.

As you have read earlier in the book, commodity cycles typically run a good 20 years. There has never been one that lasted for under 15 years. Since commodity cycles have averaged at twenty-year periods fairly consistently, this means that you have to know when a bull market cycle began in order to properly understand how much time is left in this commodities bull market cycle.

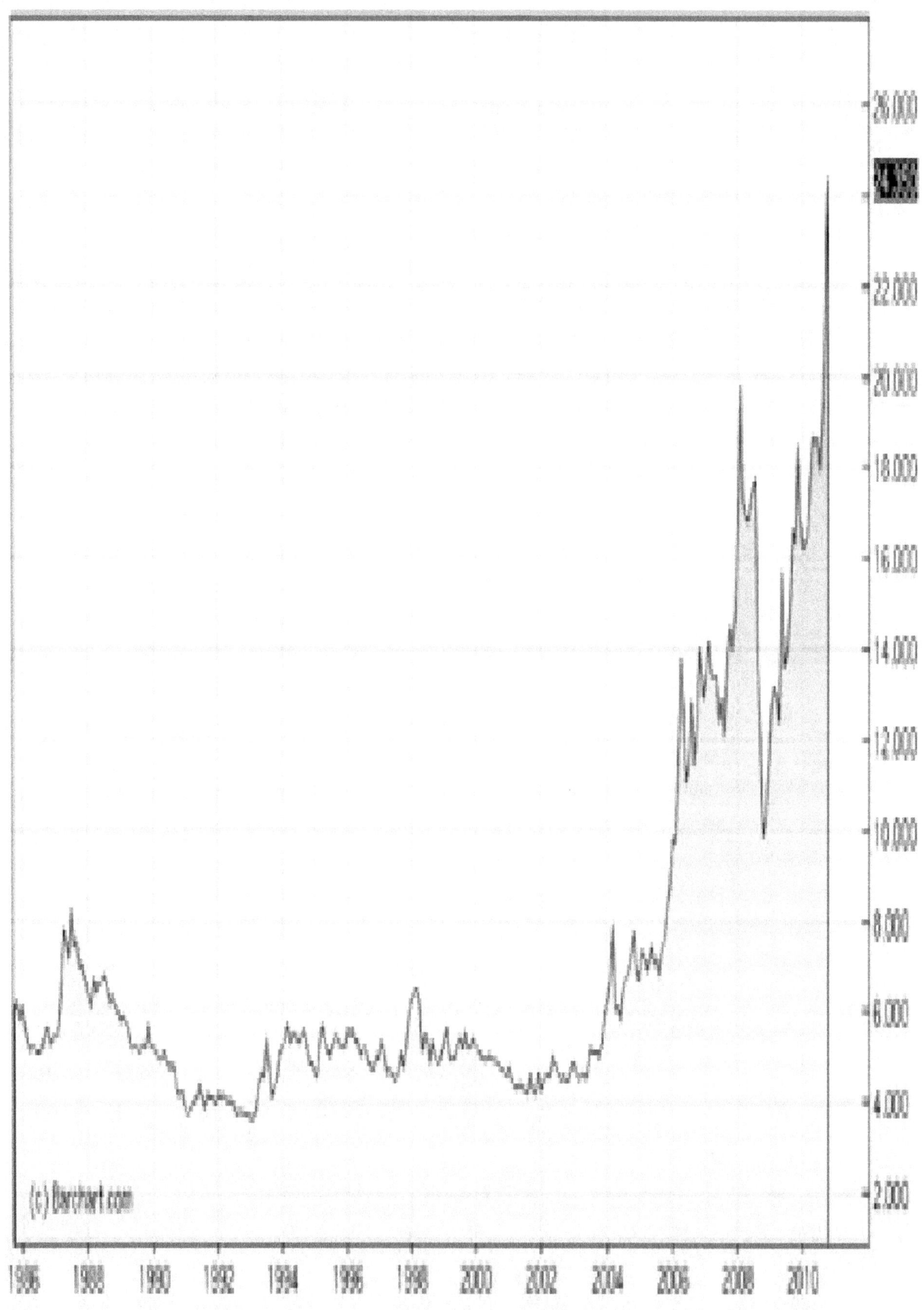

Above chart shows the Silver trend from 1986 - 2010

Prices for silver actually bottomed out back in the year 2001. The cumulative monthly average for silver hit its low in November of 2001 at an incredibly low $4.12 per ounce average for the month. Silver prices ended 2001 at $4.52 per ounce. From that point and year on, silver prices have been steadily increasing, having seen a closing price of $4.66 per ounce in 2002, a closing price of $5.96 in 2003, and a closing price of $6.81 in 2004.

These represented gains of three percent in 2002. Percentage wise, the bull market in silver really took off in the year 2003, as silver managed an impressive almost 28 percent gain that one year alone. 2004 proved to be strong too, with silver running up more than 14 percent.

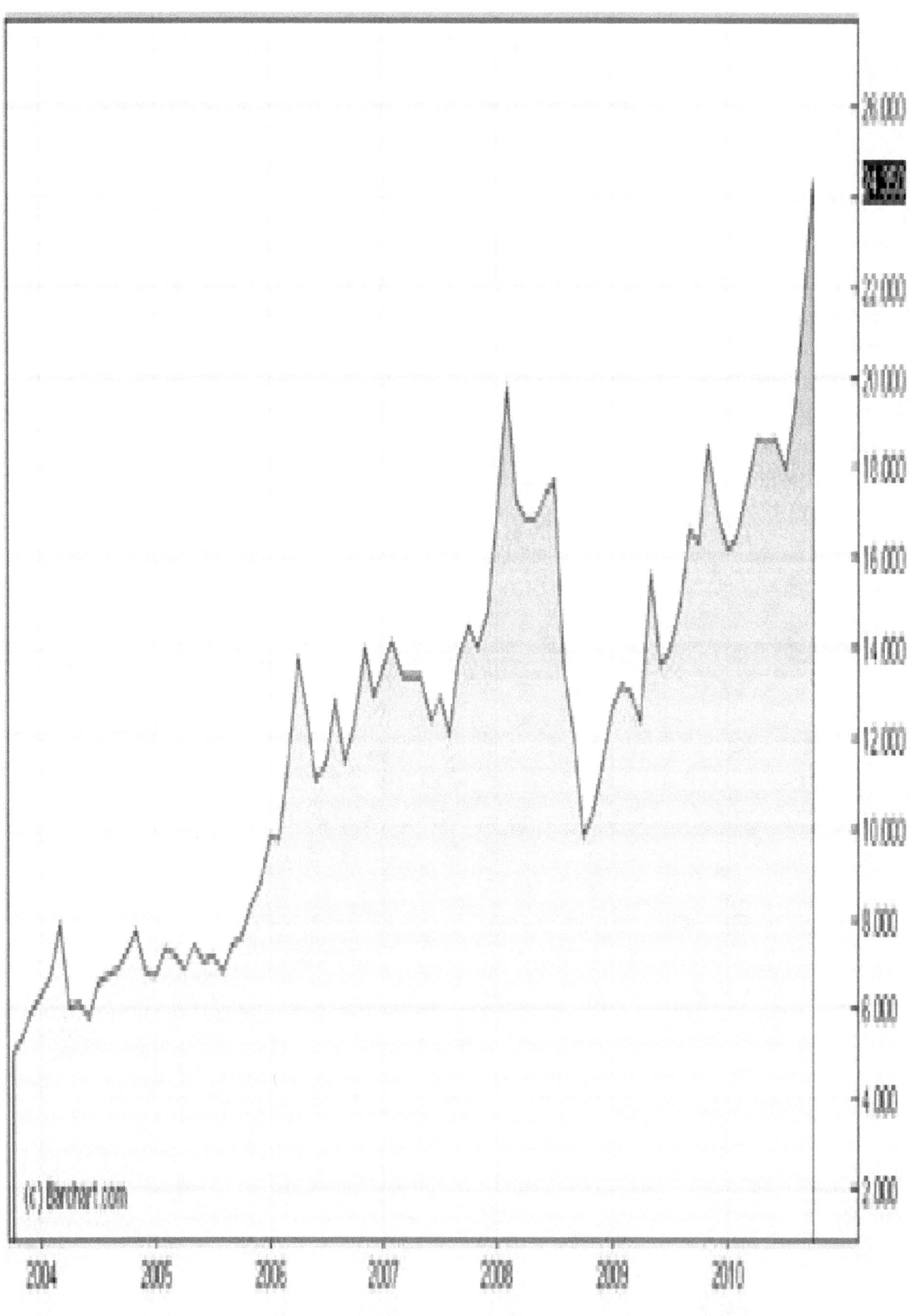

Above chart shows the Silver trend from 2004 - 2010

Silver closed at $8.83 per ounce in 2005, again closed substantially higher at $12.90 per ounce in 2006, and reached another solid high in the bull run of $14.76 per ounce in 2007. These represented annual gains of nearly 30 percent for the year in 2005. In 2006, the gains weighted in at a staggering 46 percent increase. For 2007, the year's percentage gains proved to be less torrid at a still decent 14.5 percent.

To bring silver current, you should know that in ended the year of the financial panic of 2008 at $10.79 per ounce, while finishing off 2009 at $16.99 per ounce. For 2010 as of the first week of October, silver is at over $23 per ounce. It suffered its first bull market run decline in 2008, having dropped nearly 27 percent with the world economy.

By the end of 2009, silver was back up to a new bull run high, tacking on gains of 57 percent for the year, or 15 percent since 2007. So far in 2010, silver has made another banner year, with gains through the first week of October tallying over 35 percent.

Since the bull market run began at the end of 2001, silver has gained from $4.52 to $23 plus per ounce. In ten years, this is an increase of $18.48 per ounce.

It represents a decade long gain of nearly 410 percent. Averaged over the period, this comes out to nearly 41 percent per year for ten years.

This is an impressive run for silver, but it is only for ten years. The average bull market runs 20 years, and the shortest commodities bull market has lasted 15 years. Either way, you can count on between five and ten more years of the bull market continuing in silver.

Getting back to the question asked earlier in this section about how long it would take silver to run the remaining from 117 percent, to 390 percent, to 615 percent amounts that potentially remain in site for silver based on constant dollar, gold to silver ratio dollar, and inflation adjusted dollar highs, the answer becomes simple. Silver should achieve somewhere in this range of gains over the next five to ten years.

That means for someone who invests in silver now, the silver bull market should return somewhere between around 12 and over 23 percent per year on average if the highest point reached is the constant dollar high. If the high point reached is the average gold to silver ratio number, then you could see returns of 390 percent over five to ten years, translating to as much as from 39 to 78 percent returns on average per year.

And should the inflation adjusted high for silver be reached within the remaining five to ten years of this particular commodities bull market cycle, then you could anticipate an astonishing 615 percent appreciation over five to ten years, weighing in at from 61percent per year to over 120 percent per year on average.

The one thing you can count on is that the bull market in commodities is still far from over. With at least five years left to it according to the shortest bull market in commodities ever recorded, and ten years left till the average length of bull market run ends, you have not missed out on silver's run yet. Now is the time to acquire it in one of its many forms while these amazing opportunities to grow wealthy with silver still abound.

5.3 Housing Silver Long Term and Short Term

Buying silver in physical bullion form is the first way to acquire your silver investment. Silver bullion comes in the form of coins and bars. There are advantages and disadvantages to each type.

Silver coins are beautiful to have and to admire. Silver coins can be purchased in a wide range of weights. The one ounce versions of these silver coins are the most popular with investors. There are a wide variety of these made around the world today. Australia's Perth mint makes a different animal fronted silver coin every year.

The U.S. mint has been minting Silver Buffalo coins and Silver Eagle coins for a number of years now. Both are extremely popular. Canada and Austria similarly mint beautiful silver coins every year. The advantage to buying such coins lies in the pride and joy of owning and looking at them. They are simple to store and transport as well.

The downside is that their premium cost over the actual price of silver is quite high, since they are prized by collectors for their beauty. Some of these coins can be in very high demand and command a significant premium over investment value of silver, in fact.

Silver bullion bars are the other major way to physically acquire and own silver for personal investment. They remain a popular choice for silver investors since they come with a low premium cost over the actual price of silver. Small silver bullion bars are also simple to transport and store. The larger ones, called ingots, offer the disadvantages of high storage costs and transportation problems. Because of this, you can typically have heavy silver bars at the lowest premium over silver value.

Costs for acquiring and storing such silver bullion products vary dramatically. Silver bars of 100 ounces carry low commissions of around $50 apiece. This breaks down to a reasonable 50 cents per ounce to obtain one. Ten ounce bars feature commissions of around $10 each, or about $1 per ounce. One ounce rounds or bars come with commissions of approximately $1.70 each.

With the coins, the premiums over silver cost vary wildly. Australian 2011 one ounce Rabbits can be had for around $4 over actual silver prices, while one ounce Canadian Maple Leafs and one ounce Austrian Philharmonics cost about $2 over real silver prices. American one ounce Silver Eagles premiums run around $3 and up over current silver prices.

Storing silver is a matter of personal choice. It can be kept in third-party custodian vaults at relatively high storage and insurance prices of several percent of the value of the silver. There are minimums that apply, and these usually run in the range of several hundred dollars.

A more affordable option for storing silver coins and bars is in a safe deposit box. Safe deposit boxes are kept securely in the vaults of your local bank. In most markets, these run from $100 to $150 per year for maintenance fees, although this depends on the size of the safety deposit box that your silver holdings require.

Finally, you could choose to store your silver bullion in you own home. If you opt for this choice, then you should invest in a wall safe, false cupboard, or false wall. No one should know that you have silver in your house, and it should be well concealed in one of these storage locations.

5.4 Silver ETFs in the Digital Age

Another way to benefit from silver price appreciation is through buying silver Exchange Traded Funds (ETFs) like SLV. ETFs trade on major world public stock exchanges. SLV is found on the AMEX stock market exchange right here in America. It represents the first of the different silver ETFs that came out back in 2006.

The beauty of ETFs like SLV and others lies in their trading like shares that are easily bought and sold in a familiar stock market exchange environment. The shares of silver exchange traded funds actually represent silver assets, namely silver in the actual physical form stored in vaults. While SLV only acquires actual physical silver bullion, different silver ETFs invest in other silver related assets.

Some exchange traded funds buy stock shares in silver mining companies. Others buy stock shares in companies that actually refine silver. Nowadays, there are silver ETFs that invest in literally all steps of the exploring, mining, and production processes for creating physical silver. If you are interested in these various different aspects of producing silver, then one of these may be for you.

For most investors interested in pure price appreciation possibilities for silver, SLV is the exchange traded fund to pursue. SLV shares represent an underlying one ounce ownership in silver ounces itself. You can not take delivery of the silver by owning SLV, so it is not a substitute for owning physical silver. Instead, it is a vehicle for tracking the price of silver. The goal of the ETF is to mirror the silver price performance on any given day.

The way that the custodians of SLV accomplish this is by equalizing their holdings of silver as the holders of the shares buy or sell more of them. When the supply and demand pressure on SLV threatens the ETF with breaking away from the underlying metal price, the managers step into the market to acquire or liquidate physical silver holdings.

For example, if the stock market traders buy up SLV shares and bid the price up faster than the metal is moving, the custodians will issue more shares to control the price and use the cash proceeds to buy more silver ounces. If on the other hand, SLV shares are being sold at a greater rate than silver itself is, the custodians purchase back SLV shares by selling a portion of their actual silver bullion holdings.

In this way, they keep the price of the SLV shares consistent with that of actual silver ounces itself. This means in general that the price of SLV and silver itself are approximately the same.

Another advantage to owning shares in the SLV ETF vehicle for those who are not interested in having physical silver in their holdings lies in the use of margin and leverage. Because SLV trades like a stock, most brokerages will allow you to buy more SLV shares than you actually have funds for in your account.

Assuming that you meet their margin requirements, you can buy as much as two times the amount of SLV as you have dollars. For example, with the SLV trading at $22 per share, you might acquire 100 shares, representing 100 ounces, for $2,200. If you had authority to trade margin in the account, you could benefit from the two to one leverage provided by it.

This means that you would be able to purchase 200 shares, representing $4,400, worth of the SLV, even though you only had $2,200 in the account. The advantage to this is that while silver is moving up, your investment is growing twice as fast with the leverage as it would be without it. For every one dollar increase in the price of SLV, your account value will gain $200 instead of only $100.

The disadvantage is exactly the reverse. If SLV falls one dollar per share, then your account value will drop $200 instead of only $100. Leverage and margin can be powerful tools to significantly increase your buying power of SLV and the underlying silver with it but they entail some risk.

5.5 Leveraging ETF AGQ for 100% More Gain

Another exchange traded fund vehicle for acquiring silver ounces is the ETF AGQ. AGQ is the Pro Shares Ultra Silver ETF. The AGQ Pro Shares Ultra Silver ETF trades on the New York Stock Exchange, helping to make it extremely liquid. This investment offers a tremendous advantage for you readers who wish to acquire a more significant exposure to silver.

This is because it seeks to offer twice the leverage present in individual silver ounces. In other words, these shares move at a percentage change that is twice that of silver.

For example, when silver ounces are up two percent, the AGQ Pro Shares move up around four percent. This doubling effect works both ways, once again. If silver is down one percent per ounce, then the AGQ Pro Shares will fall two percent roughly. This ETF investment gives you a two to one leverage with your silver investment money.

Once again, since this is an ETF that trades like a stock on a stock market exchange, you will have the ability to use still more leverage in the silver trade. A margin account will allow you to buy twice as much of the AGQ Pro Shares ETF as you have money for in your investment account. So instead of having simply two to one leverage on silver as you would with cash only purchases of the shares, you gain a four to one leverage by using your margin funds ability.

As an example, when silver ounces rise two percent, and you purchase AGQ Pro Shares on margin, then you can once again expect a four percent rise in the AGQ Pro Shares. Your account would be up eight percent though, as a result of the miracle of leverage.

Once again, you should remember that this leverage power cuts too ways, and make sure you have the ability to withstand moves to the downside in silver, as these do occur along the way. If the AGQ Pro Shares are bought on margin, and silver falls one percent in value, then the AGQ ETF value will similarly fall two percent. On margin though, this would translate to a four percent drop in your account value.

The thing that you have to remember when purchasing things on margin is that you must have enough funds in your account to withstand temporary price changes that move against you. Silver dropping only three percent is not so bad when you have purchased the silver shares with cash.

The AGQ ETF falls six percent, which is bearable. But a one day 12 percent drop in your account value because of margin may put you in a situation with your brokerage house in which it wants you to send in more money to keep the position open. Different brokers have different minimum requirements, but many of them will require that you keep at least a third of the value of your margined position in account value.

This means that if you have $10,000 in margin purchased securities, the account will then have to maintain a minimum $3,300 value or they will call you and ask for you to deposit more funds. If you can not or will not deposit more funds and quickly, then they will sell your position immediately, and you will lock in the loss, no matter how steep or temporary it might prove to be.

Because of this, it is wise to be careful when using margin accounts and leverage. This is particularly the case when the leverage starts to be higher because of the leverage inherent in the silver ETF.

Tools like leverage and margin accounts can be a terrific way to increase the amount of silver that you control, so long as you have enough stay in power to ride out the day-to-day and week-to-week bumps along the bull market trend path. Silver may be going up fairly consistently year on year, but it does not necessarily go up consistently every day, week, or even month along the way.

5.6 Silver Numismatics – Not Just a Coin Toss

There is another way to invest in silver that takes advantage of the rarity and popularity associated with the investment vehicle. This is through numismatic coins. Numismatic coins are different from the bullion coins explored along with bullion bars earlier in the chapter.

Numismatic coins refer to those that are sought out by numismatists, or collectors, because of their beauty and possible rarity. When you purchase a numismatic coin as opposed to a bullion coin, then you are buying a collectible coin for more than just its underlying silver value. You are buying it hoping that it will become rare over time as more and more collectors seek to acquire it.

Since the American Eagle Silver dollar coin was designed and released almost 25 years ago back in 1986, these American Eagles have turned into the most widely collected and beloved coin in all of American minting history. This is partly because many collectors consider the coin's design to be among the most lovely, if not the loveliest of American coins ever made.

The coin's front showcases the Walking Liberty design that was first employed on U.S. Silver Half Dollars from World War I to World War II. The back of the coin highlights a heraldic eagle. The silver in this one ounce coin proves to be .999 pure. The coin itself is around 1.6 inches in diameter.

Because of this, any prior year Silver Eagle dollar coin will likely be sold to you at a significant premium over the actual value of silver on any given day. How much of a premium depends on the year at which you are looking. Some years prove to be more popular with collectors than others do. This is just a function of how many such Silver Eagle dollars are struck in a given year, and how in demand they turn out to be.

As an example, the Silver Eagle dollars from 1999 to 2010 are all available at the same price. The 1997 sells at an almost five dollar premium over the last ten years plus issues though. The 1996 version sells for $30 premium over the more recent years. The 1986 sells at a five dollar premium, as does the 1997 year. You can not be sure when you buy these numismatic coins for how much higher than the actual silver value that they will trade. But it does give you an additional possibility of realizing profits besides only the underlying silver price increase.

Silver Eagles are interesting because they are hybrids between numismatic and bullion coins. When they are issued new from the U.S. mint, they are offered at a reasonable four to five dollars premium over silver. Most any new bullion silver coin from around the world will cost you that same premium over actual silver price.

With Silver Eagles, not only do you gain direct exposure to silver prices ounce per ounce, but you similarly gain the possibility of the most popular U.S. minted coins in history gaining in numismatic value. This makes these vehicles of owning silver well worth considering in your quest to acquire the gray metal silver.

5.7 Silver Collectors – The Rare Made Valuable

As you saw in the last section, Silver Eagles are bullion coins that can have some popularity or rarity value premium added to them. If you are interested in this second factor contributing to value, then collector coins may be the best means for you to obtain your silver.

Collector silver coins naturally have value based on the underlying silver price, or intrinsic value of the silver within them. They also have the second component of value which is based on how old the coin is. The age of the coin contributes to its rarity factor.

A collectible silver coin's value has much to do with how common or rare it is. The more available an older silver coin is, the lower its collectible value will turn out to be. There are a number of such silver collectible coins that are so hard to come by that the rarity value will prove to be substantially greater than the intrinsic value of the silver. Other silver coins that are collected turn out to be so easy to find that their value is only slightly above the intrinsic silver value.

For example, if you are thinking to buy into collectible silver coins as a means of investing in silver only, then you should focus your efforts on obtaining common dates of Washington quarters and Roosevelt dimes made in 1964 and before that are in only circulated condition.

Such coins must be minted in1964 or earlier because they were made with 90 percent silver up to that point, before the government debased the silver coinage. Pre-1965 Washington quarters are comprised of 0.18084 ounces of silver, nearly a fifth of an ounce, while such Roosevelt dimes are made of 0.07234 ounces of silver, close to a tenth of an ounce.

If you decide that you have a greater interest in owning silver than simply investing in the silver content, you can pursue rarer silver collectible coins. Among these are Seated Liberty silver coins, Barber half dollars, and Morgan dollars.

You would be best served to pick out only one or two of these types of silver coins and learn as much as you can about them from a reliable coin guide. You would want to learn about the quantities of each date and mint that were produced, so that you know which dates and mint locations are rarer and which ones are more common.

You will want to compare the prices of these coins and yet always be aware of the rarity of the date and the mint location where they struck the coin. With a little practice and attention to detail, you can get the most competitive price on the rarest coin in the series. Collectible coins offer you more potential in a given silver coin that only intrinsic silver value.

5.8 Silver Mining Stocks – Don't Dig for Dollars

If you are familiar with the stock market, then you are probably wondering why the subject of silver mining stocks has not come up in this chapter. We personally do not recommend silver mining stocks as the best way to obtain exposure to silver ounces. Even though silver mining companies do own, mine, refine, and produce silver, there are several reasons why they are not the best means of obtaining your silver.

The main problem with owning silver mining stocks is that you do not gain a literal correlation to the underlying price movement with such a stock. Whether you have conglomerate mining stocks that produce silver, such as BHB Biliton, junior exploration companies, or gold and silver only mining company stocks, such as Buenaventura, this is the case. The conglomerates, for example, mine many different metals, such as copper, lead, zinc, iron, silver, and gold. The price of only silver does not impact their values much, if at all.

The next category of silver mining stocks are junior exploration companies, These are firms that have properties with unproven silver reserves that they hope to develop. Their values are more dependent on the companies' capabilities of attracting investors or selling the projects which they are working on to another company.

Literal silver mining only companies are hard to find, since silver is most commonly mined with a variety of ores from which it must be separated. Ones that produce silver almost exclusively would be the best bet for a silver mining stock in terms of its stock value correlation to silver price movements. As silver prices rise, so will their stock values. The difficulties with the investment lie in the companies. As these companies' affairs are doing well, then the stocks become cash registers.

The problem with such silver mining only companies is that they can fall victim to a number of problems that have nothing whatsoever to do with the actual price of silver. There might be strikes of the mineworkers, rising costs of raw materials, accounting problems, stronger local currencies where the silver is produced, or mine collapses. Mining companies the world over are struggling with rising production costs as they bring their silver to market.

Even the most successful of such mining companies can be hostage to prices of gasoline and oil, tires, and steel. In the midst of the bull market, this can lead to a good silver mining company under-performing Wall Street's expectations. When this happens, the share price will not move up with the price of silver, but down with the investors' disappointment.

There are simply too many factors beyond your control with mining companies. Many of them have nothing to do with the price of silver and its annual performance. This is the main reason that you should steer clear of silver mining companies when investing in silver.

Chapter 6

7 Steps to Create a Successful Investor Mindset

"Don't wait until everything is just right. It will never be perfect. There will always be challenges, obstacles and less than perfect conditions. So what. Get started now. With each step you take, you will grow stronger and stronger, more and more skilled, more and more self-confident and more and more successful."

—Mark Victor Hansen

There are seven steps to creating a successful investor mindset. In this chapter, you will read about them. Take them to heart, as they can make all of the difference in the world for you and your future when it comes to your personal investment success.

The key to their application is turning your mind into an asset. By doing so you attune it to the physical world and opportunities begin to present themselves. Become really good at it and your wishes will be answered in an almost magical fashion. Your mind is the single most powerful tool you possess when it comes to investing. It is capable of focusing on and creating the blueprint of what you want to create. This is perhaps 95 percent of what goes into successful trading itself – a focused mind making focused decisions that create what you desire.

6.1 How to Crash and Burn with Instant Gratification

Instant gratification is the most dangerous mental pattern to successful investing. It inhibits and prevents you from developing the mindset you need to make investing a habit rather than a spur of the moment thing that only happens when circumstances permit it.

How did we become a generation that wants things now, no matter what? It seems as if instant gratification is ingrained in us. The recent economic downturn has made us aware of this fact. This mindset affects virtually every aspect of our lives. Our grandparents' generation was one of savers as was that of our parents for the most part. But it seems we are a generation of spenders.

How many people do you know who are looking for the next get rich quick scheme? They are the ones that want to be shown through a video or online webinar how to get rich overnight instead of learning solid business techniques they can apply to build a successful business. They are seeking instant gratification in their professional and personal lives.

They are also the people who spend hundreds of dollars on irrelevancies like video games, hair gels, botox, and surgical procedures to give them the sense of winning (games) and the look of glamorous success if not its substance. As many of us age we seek ever more bizarre ways to retain our youth. Every gray hair and wrinkle we see in the mirror is taken as proof that at all costs, we must instantly satisfy our whims because after all, life is fleeting and needs to be consumed right now.

The problem with that belief is that deep down, we know that we are more than consumers and that instant gratification is not the answer. Many of us have come to believe that faster is definitely better and that slower is inefficient. We live in the fast lane, enjoy fast food, demand fast service, and expect fast technology yet expect timeless vigor. And we want it all now!

So How Did We Get Here?

Some people feel that technology plays an important role in this instant gratification syndrome. Technology offers a way to do more in less time. We can communicate with one another instantly through texting, e-mail, cell phones, and social networks like Twitter and Facebook.

Industry exploits our instant gratification. We are not only inundated by billboards on every highway, but besieged with advertising on every website we visit. Each message tries to stimulate us to impulse buy.

Before the current economic downturn, credit card companies offered high credit limits while realtors and financial institutions qualified homeowners for houses they could not afford. They were selling the American dream and we bought into it. Their mantra was, why wait when you can have it now? Or, buy now, pay later!

You may be living the life of instant gratification and not be aware how it is affecting your personal wealth building goals. You probably buy impulsively more than you think. The easiest easy to find out is keep track of what you buy for a thirty-day period. You may find you have an 'want mentality'. We seem to focus on what we want instead of what we really need. The only way to break the instant gratification cycle is develop a 'need mentality' instead.

Look hard at your purchases for 30 days and highlight any frivolous spending you find. Add up all the frivolous spending and take that same amount, whether it is $10 or $100, and put it in a savings account or use it to pay down debt. Get into the mindset of asking yourself, "Do I really need it?" before making any purchase at all. After a little practice, it will become second nature.

You will probably be surprised at how much extra money you have left in the bank at month's end if you simply practice this approach.

Instant gratification seems almost hardwired into our brains these days. Many of these patterns hearken back through the mists of human time when we still lived our lives in primitive caves and shelters. The time before we learned to cultivate certain plants and breed certain animals for our benefit. In those days food was not always forthcoming to our tables on a daily basis. We were hunters and gatherers. Most of the time we hunted the whole day only to come home with an empty stomach. A few berries had to calm us down before the next day started and again we had to got out and try to find food.

When we got lucky we ate everything available, consuming far beyond our normal means of sustenance. We did not know how long it would take to get lucky on the hunt again. There was only the pleasure of being sated in the moment. I believe this old mind pattern is still active within us when we do not take the time to replace this primitive response to uncertainty with a more measured one of unshakable faith in our security. This is perhaps the oldest pattern that challenges us from a part of the brain that deals with survival. We slip into this pattern when we are not fully present and aware, and nothing blows present awareness away more than trying to gratify needs that substitute pleasure for survival.

Have you ever shopped on an empty stomach? It doesn't really matter if you find yourself in a food market or a clothing store. On an empty stomach, you are considerably more predisposed to buy much more than you had originally planned. Every deal looks good, every item tempting. You are substituting the pleasure of gratification at the expense of mental clarity. Do not make the mistake of instantly grabbing the deal that looks good to you. These days everybody seems to have the best deal and they all urge you to act now or lose out. That's not the case at all.

Never buy anything on an empty stomach. Now apply that to investing. Warren Buffet looks at thousands of deals per year and his goal is to find just one good one! You can bet he is well fed and capable of clear thinking when he does this.

So take your time, use your brain and analyze a situation or a deal as long as you need to gather all necessary data and only then, when you feel comfortable with what you know, make a decision and take action.

6.2 Avoiding a Rigged Game

You should always remember that investment companies do not operate out of charitable intentions or only the goodness of their hearts. They are only managing money with the intention of being compensated for it. Their goals are to make as much money for themselves, or alternatively for their shareholders, as they possibly can. This means that they are being generously compensated by you for managing your money. They are making money off of you, and not for you. Successful investors know that by taking charge of their own money, they can cut out these middle man fees.

Investment advisers and their investment companies are fond of telling you that they are working hard to ensure your financial future. The truth is that they literally prove to be among the biggest obstructions to the building up of your wealth and preserving it. How much do investment companies actually charge to manage your money and silver investments on your behalf? The number will astonish you.

Over a span of 20 years worth of investing time, if you are an average investor who is judiciously saving for your retirement, you can count on paying the typical full service big brokerage investment firm more than $100,000 in fees and commissions. The news gets worse as the time frame extends. For 30 years of retirement savings and investments, the fees and commissions will amount to around $300,000.

The reason that you do not see these exorbitant fees is that many of them come right off of the returns that you have made. This means that they do not show up on your brokerage account statement along with the fees that you think that you are paying them. These enormous fee amounts are not for wealthy investors either, but for typical middle class investors. The amounts can be even higher if your account is involved in a "wrap fee" generated by a full service advisory account, or if your broker is churning you through many positions on a regular basis.

Another reason to avoid the big investment companies is that their advice has usually proven to be self-serving at your expense in the past. You may remember that not so many years ago, there were many charges leveled and law suits filed against the major brokerages that had been promoting products to their customers that they knew were poor investments and would fail. Why should you trust your hard earned investment dollars to people who have done this in the past, since they could easily do it again in the future?

In today's day and age, it is easy to be your own investment adviser. This is particularly the case where investments such as silver are concerned. Since all of the information that you need on the precious metal is readily available on the Internet in products like this e-book, there is no longer much mystery surrounding an investment that is so basic to comprehend as is silver. If you have your investment money with a full service broker, then do yourself a favor and stop lining their pockets. Take control of your investment dollars today, in particular your silver investment dollars. You will be glad that you did.

6.3 Personal Responsibility Equals Success

There is nothing so empowering as taking control of your money and investments. It gives you a feeling of a real stake in the investments that you pursue when you do this. Gaining control of your investments is easier than ever now thanks to the widespread accessibility of the Internet. Regaining control of your money can be done by following the ensuing advice.

The first thing that you will need to do is to fire your investment broker. There are two ways that you can get the money from them in order to start managing it yourself. If you are willing to have them liquidate all of the positions in your account, then by all means do so and have them mail you a check.

A faster way of getting your money back is to request a wire to your bank account. There are downsides to leaving your investment broker in this method. Maybe you do not want to exit all of your positions, particularly if some of them are underwater and you are waiting for them to recover. Besides this, selling them all will incur a possibly significant set of commission charges, which is the reason that you are leaving them in the first place.

A better way to do this is to set up your new investment account that you will self direct. There are a wide variety of these self-directed account companies operating today. E-trade, TD Ameritrade, and Scott Trade are just a few of the better known ones. These discount self-directed brokerages all provide low fee trades along with investment information, charts, and other helpful tools to help you make wise decisions for your investment dollars.

All of these also offer the convenience of online account portals. You can manage your investments directly from any computer or laptop and Internet connection. Nowadays, smart phones can even be used to perform some account functions, such as giving orders to buy and sell.

Once you have done this, you can simply arrange to have your assets transferred over from the full service investment company to your new self directed investment account. This is done using an automated process called the ACATS, or Automated Customer Account Transfer Service.

The NSCC, or National Securities Clearing Corporation runs this to ensure the smooth transferring of customer accounts and assets from one broker to another one. Most any commonly held assets can be simply and easily transferred. This includes bonds and stock of domestic companies, cash, and options. All that is required to start this process is to fill out a Transfer Initiation Form (TIF) and to give it to the investment company from which you will transfer your assets.

Regarding how long it will take to move your account assets over to the new self directed investment account, there are several processes involved. First the customer account information has to be matched up between the delivering firm and the receiving firm in a validation process. After this has happened, the firm that is responsible for the delivery will take another three days to move the account and assets over in what is known as the delivery process. Between the validation and delivery processes, typically six business days are involved, or a little over a week.

6.4 The Long Haul

Another precept of building wealth that you have to internalize revolves the time frame in building up wealth through investing. This is not something that happens overnight, like going on a gambling junket to Las Vegas, or winning the lottery. Investing and building up wealth takes time to accomplish. It involves a long term commitment.

Part of the long term commitment comes from needing to educate yourself on ways to save and invest your money effectively. This is a skill that has to be developed. Continuously educating yourself through reading books and articles is a necessary part of making this happen. Over time, your knowledge will grow, and your investment skills will improve as a result.

Another part of the commitment involves learning what investments work best for you. This is usually not a process of simply finding one kind of investment. Diversification is a principle that teaches you to divide up your money into a variety of different kinds of investments.

This way, when one of your investments, such as stocks, is down, another one of them, like silver, will be up. In such a way, your portfolio will be balanced out and insulated from the shocks of sudden and precipitous drops in value. Diversification is a practice that requires study, patience, and time to do well. Becoming good at it does not happen overnight.

Something else that you will have to understand is that building up wealth takes requires time to achieve. Companies or investment advisers promising you get rich quick schemes are not usually offering you a legitimate or level investment opportunity. Instead, they are generally selling high risk investments that will likely leave you with little to nothing from your original investment. The phrase grow rich slowly is one that you will have to get your head around.

Successful investing does not typically provide you with multiple digit returns. The lower and steadier returns in the eight to 15 percent range are actually very good ones for most investors. They will certainly not make you wealthy overnight. For example, if you manage to achieve even ten percent a year on average consistently, then you will still need nine to ten years before you double your investment money.

Once you adjust your mindset to the fact that building up wealth and investing will take some time, it will become easier for you to pace yourself along the process of learning, discovering what investments work for you personally, and consistently working to achieve solid and reasonable consistent returns year in and year out.

6.5 Skin Your Knees, Bruise Your Elbow, Get Back on that Bike!

Everything you learn in life involves a learning curve. The more time and effort you invest the better you become. Make your learning fun and do not focus so much at the outcome first. Enjoy the ride itself as you learn and teach yourself how to deal with finances and investments.

Teaching yourself about finances will help you to solve problems. Problems are nothing other than holes of information that you want to fill. A problem is a challenge that requires you to take a deeper look; find more information and in the end you can make a decision. Looking at problems as challenges that simply require more information to overcome is great mental training that will sharpen your thinking over time and lead to more awareness on many levels. By cultivating the habit of looking deeper, you will discover that you can hold your attention over a longer periods of time while remaining calm when problems arise.

Think about your childhood, when you learned to ride a bike. In the beginning it seemed almost impossible. You got yourself on the bike only to find that you were tipping over. Maybe your parents helped you to stay on the bike and supported you as you learned to find your balance. Every time fell off the bike you had to start over again. And it probably took a few days until you were able to hold your own balance for more than a second or two.

If at any point you had given up you would not be able to ride a bike today. It takes one attempt more to get up on the bike than it does to fall down. This one time more is the key to success. So remember this when you do your silver trading. Stick with it, constantly educate yourself, keep your balance, and you will succeed.

Before you start with silver trading set yourself a long term goal for the next several years. What do you want to accomplish in ten years with your trading? How much profit do you want to make? From that ten year goal work yourself backwards year by year to the current moment. Set a goal for every year and a goal for every month in the first year. Remember that you will make more money with more investment. So calculate that into your yearly goals. One easy way to do this is to add 50 percent or 100 percent to the amount of profit you hope to achieve every year.

6.6 It's All About Plot, Character Development, and Self-understanding

Something that holds many people back from investing effectively and successfully is the mistaken belief that finance is a boring subject to have to study and embrace. In reality, nothing could be farther from the truth. Finance explains the way that the world around you works, and it has a lot to do with your money and future. It is much like reading a novel.

A novel may start out a little dull, but once you get a little ways into it, it becomes suspenseful and gripping as you learn more about and become invested in the various characters. In the same way, finance can take some getting into, but once you begin to understand the various components of it, it starts to draw you more and more into the subject.

The first reason that finance proves to be the most interesting topic is because it is intensely relevant to your own life. Personal finance covers topics such as making a budget, saving your money, investing your money, and spending your money wisely. It includes all aspects of gaining and managing your funds. Learning more about finance will enable you to stretch your money farther and to save for the future. It will help you to lead a happier, more successful, and more rewarding life as well.

Finance is also interesting because it explains the way that many things work in the world. Businesses rely on finance to help them to operate a money making and sustainable venture. Such firms must have ways to raise money, either through issuing stocks to investors for cash proceeds, or through obtaining loans in the form of bonds.

Banks rely on finance in order to obtain deposits from consumers like you that they can turn around and loan out to businesses for expansion and cash flow purposes, or to consumers for home improvement projects or to purchase a home or a car. Finance explains how these investments work for the benefit of investors, consumers, and businesses together.

Finance is also interesting as it helps to explain the way that the national economy, of which you are a part, actually works. Public finance looks at the ways that the government, through such intermediaries as the Federal Reserve Bank or the Treasury, impacts the economy through their policies such as monetary, interest rate, and credit policies.

Learning about this topic of public finance will enable you to understand the impacts that the various government policies are practically having on your investments. It will also help you to recognize opportunities for future investment ideas.

The more that you learn about finance, the more interesting it will become for you. Finance has everything to do with your personal life, efforts of investing, and ability to build up wealth. You will find that it will draw you in, like that big thick novel, if you only give it a chance and some time.

6.7 Grok It Fully Before You Go for It

As an investor you need to understand your investment. You need to know exactly what you are doing. There are so many investment opportunities available that it can seem very confusing in the beginning. However, when you look a bit deeper into most investment opportunities you will find out quickly that almost 99 percent of them are smoke and mirrors. They either lack a high return or they are not providing you with information on how the investment works.

Most of them get you emotionally excited, as they promise you high return in a short time. In 99 percent of all cases this is not the case, but it is possible. And a good investor will search until such a 1 percent opportunity is found. Warren Buffet, probably one of the world's greatest investors, looks at thousands of deals per year only to find one good one that he will invest in.

People that do not understand investing will always tell you to diversify because that's what they've been told by people who only imperfectly grasp the fundamentals of good investing. In my opinion even the top investment companies will give you that advice. The reason is simple – they either don't know what a good investment is or they do know but use it only to their own advantage and hide that information from you. Most financial advisors do not invest in the same opportunities that they offer their clients.

Don't be fooled by any get rich quick schemes. Professional investing requires know-how that you have to learn through experience. There are no shortcuts. If you don't learn in this way you will either lose money or someone else will make money at your expense. Before you start investing in silver check in with yourself and ask how much confidence you have. If you are still doubtful don't start investing, read this book another time or maybe take a look into the resource section on the end of this book and read some other books on investing.

I have lost thousands of dollars when I started investing in the stock market years ago. I did not know what I was doing. I almost randomly picked stocks bought and sold them. Friends gave me tips on stocks and I listened without understanding what the selected company was doing in the real world.

It is frustrating when you get up every day in the middle of the night (at that time I lived in Hawaii) and follow the stock market only in the end to lose money. It makes you want to quit for life. It took me almost a year to digest this financial debacle and I almost made up my mind that this is not for me.

When I switched from working on a Windows-based computer to a Mac I also checked the stock price of Apple once a while and I could see that Apple's stock was going up constantly. As I worked with Apple products I could see and feel the company behind them. When the iPod came out is was a revolution in the music industry – much like when Sony introduced the Walkman.

This company was listening to its customers and, a rarity these days, was and still is innovative and creative when it comes to its products. To make long story short I bought Apple stock and made profit on the sales. I would have kept my Apple stocks but by that time I had become more interested in the silver market and it was another happy change in my investment strategy. This book is a direct result of that change.

This story simply illustrates my point that you need to understand what you are doing. Information is the new money.

6.8 Keep Teaching the Dog for Laughs and Giggles

You can not overstate the importance of your financial education. It must be pursued so that your knowledge base for investing and growing your wealth will only expand and improve with time. To increase your financial education you will have to invest both time and probably money into it.

The time component that has to be invested into your financial education will be significant and ongoing. You can not expect to learn all about the worlds of finance and investment overnight. The first thing that you will need to do is to acquire a broad knowledge base.

Reading helpful books and checking out websites about personal finance and general investing are good places to start. Familiarizing yourself with all of the terms used regularly in these topics will be necessary in order for you to fully appreciate the other reading that you will do later. Besides this, you need to have a general understanding of such important sub-topics as budgeting, saving, investing, and growing wealth.

After you have secured a good knowledge base for your financial education, you will need to be continuously reading on a daily or at least weekly basis. There are many online websites or business newspapers that can help you to keep up with the most important developments in the economy and investing.

Since most of these highlights will impact your money and investments in some way or another, it is a sensible idea to be aware of them and understand their personal relevance. Where silver is concerned, there are daily and weekly price move trading explanations and analyses available, as well as the COMEX published weekly commitment of traders report.

But you should also understand the broad movements of the economy and industrial demand and output to have a larger picture of how industrial demand for silver will hold up. These are just a few of the topics that you will want to know about and comprehend.

You will similarly find that there is also a monetary cost or component involved with many kinds of financial education. While many online subscriptions are free, many of the better ones are not. For example, the Wall Street Journal charges to read their online financial newspaper, as does Barron's Online and

Forbes online. Yet the knowledge that you can gain on a daily and ongoing basis is significant and well worth a low subscription fee cost.

There are other financial costs associated with a financial education. Seminars and classes are both good ideas to help you increase your knowledge on finance and investing. Both of these avenues will move you significantly ahead in your quest for knowledge and understanding, and both of them require somewhat more substantial investments.

Seminars on money management and investing will likely cost in the hundreds of dollars. They typically run a number of hours and sometimes for a whole weekend. Classes on personal finance and investing are offered at area colleges and community colleges. These last a semester and can cost from the hundreds to the thousands of dollars.

Think of these costs as an investment in your financial well being and future, since that is exactly what they are. As your knowledge grows and you begin to take positive and proactive steps in saving and investing, you will reap a return on your investments. In the end, this will be many times the investment that you made in the financial education that got your whole wealth building process started.

Take a look at the resource section where I have listed two great websites that provide you with daily updates on the silver market.

6.9 It Seems Like an Eternity

When you first begin your process for building wealth and investing, it will likely feel that you are not getting anywhere at all. You may believe that you are spending huge amounts of time trying to learn the basics and are not really making any progress. The great thing about learning is that once you have put some time into it, you will find that the speed of the process begins to increase exponentially.

You cannot hope to know all about which investments to pursue until you understand investing in general. Learning the rudiments of investing may seem slow and tedious. It can be. But once you have cemented that basic level of understanding, then more specific investment themes will begin to fall into place.

Similarly, reading through that first book on personal finance and investing will be a slow chore in many cases. But the next articles or books that you read through will go significantly faster and easier for you. Every book or article that you read on these topics will get easier and come more naturally to you as your mind begins to truly grasp the concepts involved.

Where silver investing is concerned, you need to know many basics to investing before you will begin to feel like you are making any real progress with specifically having a handle on silver as an investment. For example, supply and demand are key concepts, as are interest rates, economic indicators, and currency movements.

Yet all of these knowledge bases must be laid before you will begin to fully understand the picture surrounding the silver market. Once you secure the learning of these fundamentals, then suddenly silver will start to make intuitive sense to you. One day, you will realize that your learning speed is rapidly increasing as all of the concepts begin to fall into place.

Learning anything new in life takes some time and dedication. Changing your overall mindset is not easy. Yet it can be accomplished with a little work and commitment.

6.10 A Little Thing Called Your Financial IQ

If you do not have enough money you have a problem. This problem can only be solved with more financial education. You can also work more and harder, however, in the long run devoting more of your time and putting more energy into your work will not solve your problem with money.

Solving problems in general increases your overall intelligence. When you solve financial problems you increase your financial intelligence. Most people that do not have enough money ignore financial knowledge. Even if you think you have financial knowledge, but you think the whole system is wrong and corrupt, you are still missing basic financial knowledge. And without financial knowledge you can have no hope of increasing your financial intelligence.

When you go all the way down to the financial rabbit hole you will come to understand that it's all a game and nothing more. Sure, money is a serious thing. Having money equates to social status and success in our society. But the moment you get too serious about it you have already lost the game, which means that you no longer have the awareness that you are operating in a game. Keep it light, keep it simple, play the game. Don't worry too much about winning and losing. Simply play the game to the best of your abilities. That's the only way to keep alive your passion for money. It's the best way to be an investor.

After solving your own financial problems you may want to think about solving other people's financial problems. They will pay you good money for solving their problems. With every financial problem you solve you increase your financial intelligence and make more money to boot. It's all part of the game.

So make it your task to solve your financial problems. If you are a bit short on money think about ways to get more. Be creative and think outside of the box. Take a walk or do something in nature, that great mother of balance and healing available to us all. Contemplate a solution to your money problems.

A fantastic way to engage your mind in financial problem solving is asking yourself a question that already implies the outcome. For example, "How do I double my money next month?" or "Why do I know I will make $20,000 profit next month with my silver investment?"

Your mind is a problem solver and a hungry one at that. When you feed it the right questions it will start working on the problem 24/7 until comes up with an answer. Involving the certainty of your belief in making it so, the answer is basically nothing less than an affirmation combined with a question. The question triggers your mind to search for a solution. The outcome or answer is your affirmation that it now has the right information to find that solution and put it to work.

Train your mind to solve problems. It is the difference between thinking and having thoughts. Thoughts are simply random bits of information that arise in your consciousness in a process that's more of less akin to simply listening to white noise or static. Thoughts alone are the byproducts of simply having a brain. Thinking on the other hand – when done powerfully, actively, openly, and in a focused way – literally has the power to create reality. Thoughts just happen. Thinking is the living, active process that powers your creations. Thinking provides the blueprint your mind needs to turn its actions into reality.

Engage yourself in mental activity and creative thinking. You may get tired easily in the beginning, but with every day you train a bit you will make progress and experience longer and more intense creative times during which you can solve problems. Take a childlike curiosity in your emerging creativity. Remember when you were a child – it used to be fun!

Chapter 7

The Nuts and Bolts of Buying and Selling Silver

"The genius of investing is recognizing the direction of a trend - not catching highs and lows"—Unknown

Now we finally come to the nitty gritty of silver investing. In this chapter you will learn the various tactics you can use to trade and profit with silver. You will learn what a margin account is and how it can help you get more leverage on your investment. You will also learn the basic formulas for how to trade and make a profit each time.

7.1 Margins and Leverage Accounts – Taming Calculated Risk 101

In the last chapters, we mentioned margin accounts briefly. Now you are going to learn how they actually work. Margin accounts can be a powerful tool in obtaining greater amounts of certain forms of stock exchange traded silver, so long as they are used with caution and wisdom.

When you hear the terms margin account mentioned, a particular brokerage account is being discussed. This kind of brokerage account permits you the owner of the account to actually borrow money to invest from your investment broker. The collateral in these types of investment loans are whatever equities and other investment holdings that you have in the account.

Setting up such a margin investment account typically requires you to read and sign a specific margin agreement that lays out the terms and conditions under which you are able to borrow the funds and under which the broker is able to collect again later.

Such margin accounts are useful as they prove to be the most common way for you to achieve leverage on your initial account deposit. This can help you to increase your profits on silver trades substantially. The broker also benefits in collecting a small interest rate on your margin loan. There is little risk of default on broker margin loans since the loans are guaranteed by the account asset value. This means that collection of the loan is easy for them.

You are likely interested to know how much margin leverage power you can obtain with such a margin account. The Federal Reserve Board sets the rules with Regulation T. They allow you to borrow as much as 50 percent of the cost of securities that you will purchase. This means that if you buy $10,000 worth of silver exchange traded funds, you would have to have at least $5,000 worth of cash in the margin account to effect the purchase.

There is also a minimum maintenance level value that has to be maintained in this margined investment. It is typically about 25 percent means that on your $10,000 worth of silver ETFs that you bought with $5,000 margin, the margined $5,000 portion has to be worth minimally $1,250. Brokers are able to change this maintenance amount at their discretion. They will notify you after they do so.

It is important to remember that there are risks associated with margin. Although it does increase your leverage by two to one, giving you the ability to double your return on silver investment profits, this comes with a greater amount of danger.

Should your account value drop below the minimum maintenance level your broker requires, your broker is able to simply sell off as many assets as needed in the account to collect on the loan. In many cases, you would first be given a chance to send in additional funds to meet this margin call, although the broker is not required to afford you this.

If the broker does go through with the asset sales, you will have no option to prioritize which get sold first. This means that your silver investment could be sold, and at a lower level than you would want to accept for it typically.

Using leverage power with a margin account to increase your silver holdings can be very profitable so long as you are prepared to ride out the dips in silver prices along the way. It is necessary for you to keep a close eye on account value with such an account and margined position.

It is possible for your account value to drop suddenly below the margin minimum to where you owe the broker more than the entire account value is worth. After the broker sells off whatever assets you had in the account, he then bills you for the rest of the money. It is fair to say that with this type of account, it is possible to lose more than the money that you deposit. This is far less likely with silver holdings, since silver will not simply drop 50 percent, as some company stocks might.

7.2 Taming Calculated Risk 102

Leverage in a margin account can be a powerful way to increase your silver holdings and resulting profits as silver prices rise. There are still more ways to margin silver using leverage, as we hinted at in previous chapters. When you buy the SLV ETF, you are gaining exposure of one share per one ounce of silver approximately. Other ETFs that track silvers performance offer greater opportunities to gain as silver prices rise. The ETF AGQ is one of these.

Some Silver ETFs achieve their holding goals by buying actual physical silver ounces, like SLV. Others invest in silver miner stocks or silver refiners' stocks. AGQ, which stands for the Pro Shares Ultra Silver ETF, buys into silver futures and forwards. It does this with a goal of matching the silver price as measured in U.S. dollars every day on the London exchange at the close of daily trading.

These futures and forward contracts allow them to buy more silver positions than they can literally afford with the cash that they have on hand. In other words, they use the power of leverage to increase the gains or losses in the exchange traded fund as silver rises or falls.

The end result is a silver ETF that moves at two times the gain or loss percentages as do actual silver ounces. You gain double the exposure to silver that you would have with silver ounces or the SLV ETF. This means that if you have $10,000 worth of AGQ, and the price of silver rises by five percent, then your AGQ value will rise about ten percent, or $1,000 in value.

It also means that if the price of silver falls by five percent, the value of your AGQ ETF will fall by around ten percent, or $1,000 in value. Two times the margin means two times the gains or losses every trading day.

ProShares Ultra Silver (ETF) (Public, NYSE:AGQ)

98.69

+4.05 (4.28%)

After Hours: **100.53** +1.84 (1.86%)
Oct 20, 7:18PM EDT
NYSE real-time data - Disclaimer
Currency in USD

Range	96.12 - 99.76	P/E ·
52 week	41.55 - 105.20	Div/yield ·
Open	96.33	EPS ·
Vol / Avg.	609,927.00/543,000.00	Shares 2.26M
Mkt cap	222.86M	Beta ·

iShares Silver Trust (ETF) (Public, NYSE:SLV)

23.33

+0.49 (2.15%)

After Hours: **23.47** +0.14 (0.60%)
Oct 20, 7:47PM EDT
NYSE real-time data - Disclaimer
Currency in USD

Range	23.00 - 23.44	Mkt cap	7.01B	Shares
52 week	14.37 - 24.06	P/E	62.69	Beta
Open	23.03	Div/yield	-	
Vol / Avg.	13.69M/15.18M	EPS	0.37	

Look a these two screenshots taken on October 20th, 2010 from the Google financial website. The first screenshot shows you the AGQ ProShares Ultra Silver ETF and the second one the SLV iShares Silver Trust ETF.

The SLV ETF closed with a plus of 2.15% and the AGQ closed with a plus of 4.28%, that's almost exactly 100 percent better. It's not every day that the AGQ matches the 100 percent, however over a given time period of a few days it does.

It is important for you to understand that ownership of these shares in the AGQ does not give you an actual silver position. You can not call up your broker or the fund manager and ask him to send you your silver ounces. You do not have a claim on silver ounces with this investment vehicle. Instead, you are only seeking to mirror the performance of silver at a rate of two to one leverage with such an investment.

If you are interested in actually owning the physical silver, or having a claim on silver ounces with your silver investment, then this is not the best investment possibility for you. But if you are looking to maximize your gains on the price movements in silver, and you can stand the ups and downs of silver along the way, then this Pro Shares Ultra Silver ETF may be the perfect investment vehicle for you.

Remember from the discussion on margin accounts that you can increase your exposure to silver from a simply two to one to four to one position by purchasing AGQ shares in your margin account with margin money.

This allows you to double your already two to one exposure by acquiring twice as many shares of AGQ as you could otherwise afford in the account. Keep in mind though, that the $10,000 investment that you had the cash for is now an up to $20,000 investment in AGQ. So five percent moves in the price of silver, that translate to ten percent moves in the silver price based ETF AGQ, will now be affecting you at the rate of 20 percent.

This means that a five percent rise in silver will make you $2,000 on your original $10,000 investment. It also means that a five percent decline in silver will cost you $2,000 of your original $10,000 investment. Remember too that these are only gains and losses on paper until you sell the investment and lock them in.

So a $2,000 loss on $10,000 looks very painful, but it has not been realized until you sell it. Similarly, a $2,000 gain on $10,000 is also 20 percent and will make you feel very happy. But, you have not gained this profit until you sell the ETF shares either.

7.3 Day Trading Revealed

Silver can also be day traded. For those of you who have heard of day trading but never understood what exactly is involved, day trading proves to be a strategy for trading securities that makes you close your positions out by the conclusion of each trading day. Engaging in day trading requires a great amount of patience, tolerance for risk, work, preparation, and study. If you succeed at it with reliable results from well developed skills, then you can bring in a significant income from it.

Day traders have to respond rapidly to the changing conditions of the market. This means that they typically purchase and then sell a given stock in even the same hour. If you do day trading, you will probably use margin trading to increase the size of your positions and the hoped for profits as you are seeking out tiny percentage gains in a security. You would attempt to make steady profits all the while managing your risk. Day trading can be done in a variety of markets, such as precious metals, stocks, options, currencies, futures, and bonds.

Day trading has ups and downs. If you develop a strategy that works, then you may make greater than 100 percent profits on a single trade in a given day. The problem revolves around keeping your investment capital without suffering terrible losses. These losses can wipe out your capital in a short amount of time if you make repeated mistakes. If you approach day trading with a gambler's mindset, then you can be financially ruined.

The idea with day trading is to be patient and wait for the right opportunity. If you engage in it, then you are only looking for a relatively small number of trades per day, perhaps from just two to twenty trades. Most of the time spent day trading involves staring at a computer screen looking for good opportunities to trade.

This working with moving stock charts more than six hours per day takes a great amount of discipline. If you are going to be successful with day trading, then you will have to be prepared to absorb regular losses, keep them small, and then move on to the next trading opportunity.

You should be prepared to study and learn about day trading techniques and skills before you become seriously involved with it. There are a variety of books and seminars offered on it, as well as websites with techniques for making it as a day trader. Practicing without committing real money upfront is always a good idea until you feel comfortable with what you are doing.

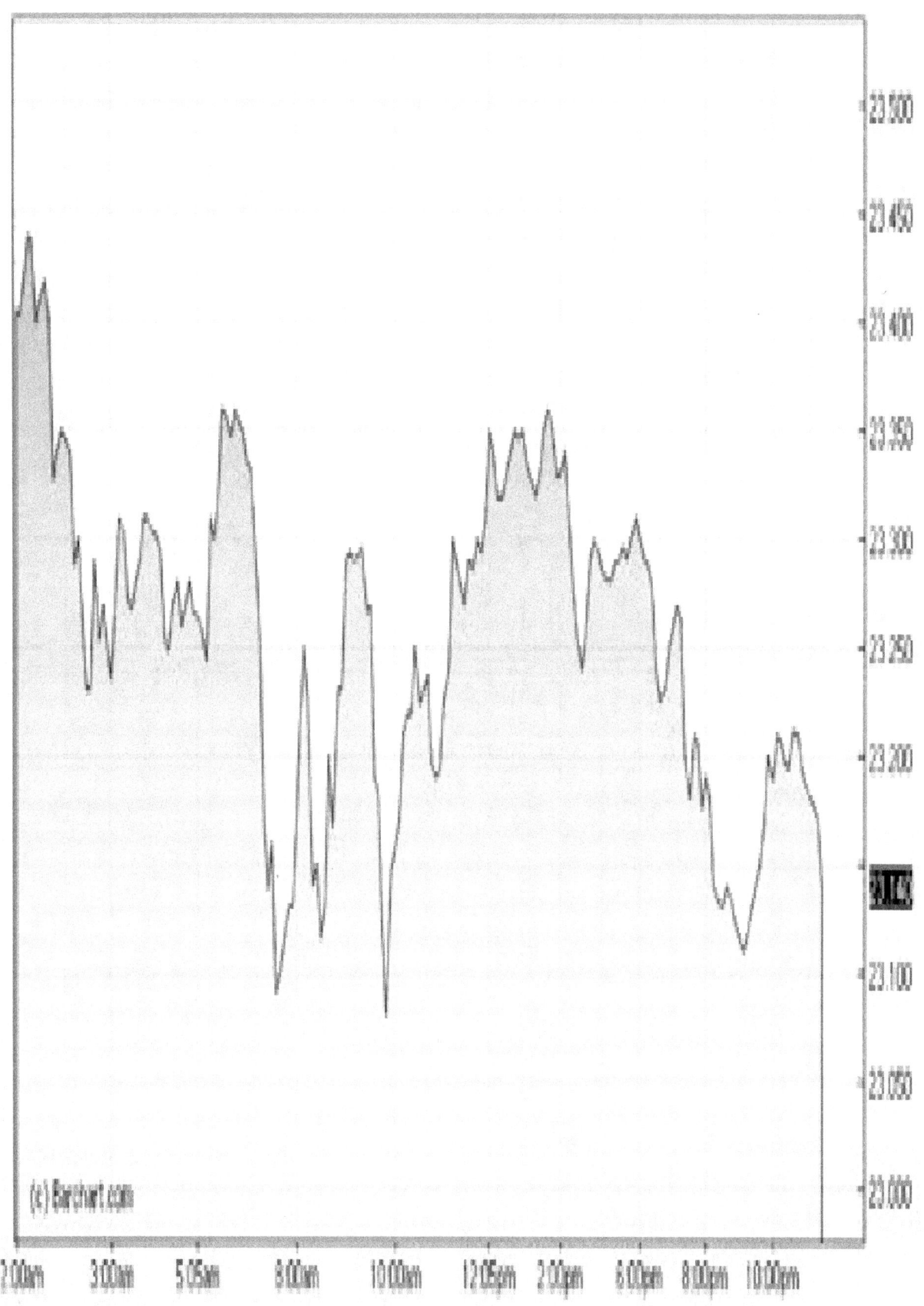

Chart above shows a usual silver intraday with a 30 cent difference between high and low

Day trading with silver can be done in one of a couple of ways. You could attempt to do it using silver ETFs, like SLV or AGQ. The problem with these vehicles is that there are not commonly large enough movements in the price of silver on a daily basis to make sufficient gains with even the eight to one margin that a margin account will get you using AGQ.

Greater margin levels can be achieved using the FOREX silver market's XAG/USD silver against the dollar position. This offers margins of 25 to 1. Trading silver futures contracts on the Commodities Exchange (COMEX) in Chicago will also give a greater margin level of fifteen to one. As both of these offer you as a day trader an ability to make greater returns on smaller moves in the underlying silver, they also can cost you greater in losses.

Studying the silver markets in depth before engaging in such day trading with the gray metal is highly recommended. You will need to learn about reading silver charts, understanding support and resistance on a daily and hourly level basis, and technical analysis of silver.

Once you have mastered these skills, you ought to open a practice account with a broker before you start trading your own real money. Then if you do decide to pursue silver day trading, be sure to start out with real money in small trades and with smart stop loss orders, or protection against losses orders.

7.4 Pattern Trading Is a Balancing Act

Trading patterns refer to the security price movement over a given period of time. Trading patterns are usually created by connecting corresponding lines of closing prices for a group of dates. A variety of stocks are effectively traded using such trading patterns. Silver can also be effectively traded using three types of pattern trading. These are seasonal patterns, commodity trading patterns, and gold to silver ratio patterns.

Seasonal patterns with silver refer to the fact that in a certain season of the year, silver is more likely to rise than at other times of the year. Put another way, at these times of the year, it is more likely to rise than to fall.

This season of commonly rising silver prices begins in September and typically runs all the way through January or even February. One of the reasons for this is because of the Indian silver and gold purchasing season for weddings. Other factors are involved too, like jewelry makers' purchasing habits.

Commodities traders also become more active coming back from long holiday breaks. When you are using this strategy of buying silver in early September and holding for the end of the year and beginning of the next, you should remember that these patterns are not 100 percent accurate. Pattern trading commodities is accurate about 54 percent of the time. This means that for about 46 percent of the time, it is wrong.

Another form of pattern trading involves commodity trading patterns as indicated in the weekly trading reports that the COMEX exchange publishes. Determining when a temporary top or bottom is near on silver can be accomplished through reading such reports. Understanding these reports is more of an art than a science. You have to comprehend how the various players in the silver market act and react to prices. The report tells you about concentrated short and long positions and how much they have changed week on week.

You can get analysis on these COMEX provided Commitment of Traders reports from various commodity trading services that will better explain to you what the level of trading activity for the various commercial hedgers, small and large speculators, and small investors all means for the current trend in the prices and future movements.

A final pattern that you can use in trading silver is the historic relationship between silver and gold. Silver has most always traded at a ratio of one to twelve against the price of gold, as we discussed earlier in the book. Since silver is trading at increasingly lower ratios, you might use these patterns to determine when the prices of silver are more severely undervalued. Lately silver has been trading at a one to fifty-eight ratio versus gold. If this gets higher, it will be even more indicative of a silver price rally.

The key to remember with pattern trading is that it is right slightly more of the time than it is wrong. The best way to make sure of making money with silver investments is to get involved with them on a longer term basis. This could likely involve a greater amount of time than simply a season or a year.

It could safely be said that the shorter the time period that you are involved with in trading silver, the harder it is to say with certainty what silver prices will actually do. Pattern trading silver is more likely to make you money than day trading silver is, and trading silver for the longer term is the most likely strategy for making money in silver investing.

7.5 When to Take It to the Bank

It is important to think about how you should manage the funds in your silver trading account. This is something that a lot of traders struggle with or do absolutely wrong. This pertains to dealing with gains that have not been realized yet, but that are showing in the trading account anyway.

If you are trading silver in a stock broker margin account either via the ETFs SLV or AGQ, this is something that you need to understand and be disciplined about. It is even more the case if you are trading silver in FOREX foreign exchange accounts or in COMEX commodities based accounts. The reason for this is that in these types of silver investment accounts, gains are literally added to the value of an account in real time.

This means that if your silver position has increased in value by $500, then the account value in either of these three account types will show a $500 gain. This is particularly the case with FOREX and Commodities accounts. In both of these accounts, gains are literally marked up to available cash the same time or day as they are recognized. This happens in real time with FOREX accounts.

The point of this is that as your silver trade profits are rising in the account, it becomes extremely tempting to take some of the money and withdraw it from the investment account to your bank account. You should never do this while the silver position is still open, just because the account value is showing a greater number than you have literally realized.

Taking money out of an investment account when gains are unrealized can be very dangerous. So long as the underlying silver position continues to rise, you will not have a problem. But if the silver position were to make a temporary top and then begin correcting back down, and you had already withdrawn the gains that you had not locked in, then you might run into trouble.

This is because of the leverage involved with these types of commodities, FOREX, and even margin accounts. Should the position start to decline in value and you not have enough cash value left in the account, then the broker of your account might decide that you are in danger of declining to a non sustainable position. Margin levels have to be maintained at a minimum, or the broker will instantly choose to liquidate the position.

For example, if the minimum value of a FOREX account that offers 25 to 1 leverage has $2,000 in it, then they will allow you to purchase $50,000 worth of silver ounces. Silver might then rise five percent, bringing your account value up to $2,500 in unrealized gains plus the original $2,000 that you deposited. This would mean that the total account value showed at $4,500.

You might then become excited about the significant gains and decide to withdraw the $2,500. This still leaves you with an account value of $2,000, you figure. But, you did not sell the silver position, meaning that your gains and losses are still marked directly to the account. If silver then reverses and drops the five percent back down, the account value will quickly decline $2,500 in value.

Before that happens though, your account value that only had $2,000 left showing in it would reach zero and your position would be closed out. This is despite the fact that silver had not changed in net value one bit from where you purchased it.

You can simply avoid these kinds of traumatic occurrences by only withdrawing funds from your silver trading accounts after you have sold your positions and locked in the gains. If you do not follow this practice, then you may actually end up losing money even though your silver trades have gone your way. There is nothing more frustrating in investing than this.

7.6 The No-no of Negative Profit

There is another important rule that goes along with the discussion in the last section. Just as you should never endeavor to withdraw money from a silver investment account until you actually sell and close out your silver position, you should never sell your silver position when you are in a losing position.

The idea behind any kind of successful investing is to buy low and sell high. If you engage in buying high and selling low instead, then you will not have many investment dollars left. If you do this sort of practice repeatedly, you will stay without any money eventually. As obvious and intuitive as this sounds, this is exactly what you are doing when you sell a silver position that is underwater, or trading below the point at which you bought it.

The next problem with selling silver positions that are in the minus column from where you bought them is that you are typically doing this from an emotional and fearful point of view. Go back and read the earlier chapters of this book in order to review the fundamentals of silver. Just because the price of silver has dropped in the short term a little from where you bought in, have any of the incredibly bullish underlying factors supporting silver changed? The answer will likely be a resounding no.

So what has changed from the point when you bought the silver to when it becomes a losing position is only your emotional state and your overall level of confidence. Confidence and emotions can get you into trouble with any kind of investing. That is why so many investment gurus will tell you that in order to be a successful investor, that you must find a way to take emotions out of the investing equation.

If you trade based on emotions, then you will likely end up losing most of the time. Either you will suddenly doubt your entire premise because the investment is temporarily moving against you, or you will refuse to sell for a good profit because you believe it can only keep going on up.

As an example of not letting your emotions rule your investment making decisions, consider the wisdom of another legendary silver and gold commodities investor named Jim Sinclair. He likens having investments in silver and gold to owning insurance. Just because you are feeling healthy or safer and secure on a given day is not a good reason to decide to sell your insurance and take a loss on it. Insurance is something that you only sell when you no longer need it, or when its value has gone up. It is the same with gold and silver

Jim Rogers, whom you have read about at various points in the book, says that he never sells precious metals like gold and silver. Certainly, he would never sell one of them for a loss. You must develop nerves that can withstand the day-to-day moves in silver if you are going to invest in it for any period of time.

You might also have to remind yourself on a daily basis that silver goes up and silver goes down, but the long trend of silver is your friend. This long term trend of this metal is soundly and solidly up. Panicking because your silver investment is underwater will only lead to losses, as well as a bitter sense of regret as you watch it recover and then move on up to make new highs in the future. Make this advice your mantra, and repeat it day in and day out. Never sell your silver position when you are underwater.

7.7 More Leverage with Option Trading

Besides these other ways of trading silver in an effort to capitalize on the phenomenal gains in store for the gray metal in the future, these is another means to gain highly leveraged exposure to silver. This is known as trading silver using options. Silver trading with options is a powerful leveraged way to control significant amounts of silver while limiting the risk associated with the high leverage.

The easiest way to get involved with options on silver is to use the AMEX traded ETF SLV as discussed earlier in the book. Remember that SLV has a goal of actually following the silver price. So options on SLV will be based on the actual price of silver, making these contracts simple to understand. They are also heavily traded, proving to be the most actively bought and sold options on any ETF that is related to silver. These options allow you to control one hundred shares of SLV ETF per single contract.

It is important to understand that these call options give you the right but not the obligation to buy one hundred shares of the iShares Silver Trust Fund SLV. These hundred share increments of the contracts make them user friendly. You are able to simply amend the call purchases to satisfy the amount of risk that you wish to take. Besides this, they give you a full one hundred to one leverage on your investment dollars which is always easy to comprehend, since each contract controls one hundred shares.

A real tangible example will help you to better grasp the potential gains and losses involved in such SLV call options. To work with actual numbers, you will examine the October 6th closing prices for SLV and the options based upon it. The advantage to call contracts lies in their ability to give you a potentially unlimited gain opportunity, while ensuring that you do not lose any more money than you put into the investment.

Take the November 19th $22 strike price calls, which might have been purchased at $1.31 per share, or $131 per call. With only a single call contract, you put just $131 at risk; this is the most that you can lose if the trade does not go your way. Because your call has a strike price of $22, it starts to gain actual value at that amount.

The break even on the option is this $22 strike price plus the $1.31 per share, or

$23.31 per share of SLV. To look at a sample of the possible gains, consider what would happen if silver prices appreciated to $25 per ounce by the day your contract expired on November 19th. The option price would be at $3.00, which would then make the option contract worth $300. The profit in this case would be $169 for the single contract, or $845 if you had five contracts.

There are more sophisticated ways of trading silver using options as well. These can be accomplished using options on COMEX silver futures contracts. These strategies are known as option spreads.

The first means of accomplishing this is in utilizing a Bullish Debit Spread. The way this works is similar to the SLV example above, only instead of being based on SLV shares, these options are based on silver futures contracts.

With a bullish debit spread, you are simply trying to reduce your out of pocket expenses on the options. The way that you do this lies in first buying a Comex silver contract call option whose strike price is equal to the literal price of the silver contract. Then, to reduce your costs and possible loss on the trade, you can sell a different silver call that has a higher strike price.

This money that you receive for selling the second call brings down the amount of money that you have spent to acquire the first option. The most that you can lose is restricted to the net amount of money that you have paid. The downside is that the profit potential is limited by the option that you sold. No additional gains will be made above its strike price.

Look at a real priced example based on October 6th prices. On this day, the silver futures prices were at $23.18. You could have purchased the $23.00 strike priced December call for .984. These contracts are based on five thousand futures contract amounts, so the cost for this purchase would have amounted to .984 times the five thousand contracts, for $4,920 for the one option. At the same time, you would sell the $24.00 strike priced December call for .595. This would have given you .595 times five thousand contracts for $2,975. Subtracting the sold call of $2,975 from the bought call of $4,920, you would have paid a net amount of $1,945 plus all commissions.

The most that you can lose is this $1,945 net that you put into the trade. With silver futures prices below $23.00 per ounce on November 24th, this is what you would lose. Since your net cost was .389, the break even point on this trade would come in at $23.39 for the silver futures.

Anything above this would be a gain all the way up to $24.00 per silver contract. At $23.50 per silver contract, the profit would be $550 less any commissions. At $24.00 or above per silver contract on expiration date, the maximum profit would reach $3,055, which is $5,000, based on the $1.00 difference between your two call options' strikes times five thousand contracts, minus the upfront cost of $1,945.

You also do not have to wait until the November 24th expiration to sell the options. If silver experienced a significant gain ahead of time, you could sell the two options of the Bullish Debit Spread and take a significant part of the profit.

For example, on October 5th and 6th the December silver futures contract increased an incredible 65.6 cents. In this particular spread with $23 and $24 strike price calls that cost $1,920, or .384, there was a rapid profit of 19.5 cents, translating to .195 times five thousand contracts for $975. This is a not bad over 50 percent gain for two days time frame.

With these spreads, you can adjust the point where you buy the second call to put more money at risk for more potential return. Buying the $23.00 silver contract while instead selling the $24.50 one would have cost you $2,645 on October 6th, leading to a break even point of $23.53, while giving you a potential maximum profit of $4,855 at or above $24.50.

There is another way to use these COMEX options to take positions that benefit from the rising silver prices. A Bullish Credit Spread works much like the just finished example with calls. The main difference is that this strategy works with put option contracts. Put options give you the right but not the obligation to sell silver futures at a certain fixed price.

Starting this strategy would have you selling a December put option that was in the money, or with a strike price that was located above the current silver futures price. At the same time, you would have to purchase a put that had a lower strike price in order to limit your risk to a certain amount. The extra money that you get for selling the first put that is above the futures price minus the money that you pay for buying the second put is your maximum potential gain.

You receive this so long as the prices of silver futures rise over $24.00 by expiration. This would mean that both of the puts expired worthless, leaving you with the full net credit gain.

Once again working with the October 6th futures prices, you can look at the following example. While the prices of December silver futures contracts stood at $23.18, you could sell the $24.00 strike December put and receive $1.552, which when multiplied by five thousand contracts amounts to $7,760. At the same time, you would purchase the $23.00 strike priced put for a cost of 94.1 cents that translates to $4,705, when multiplied by the five thousand contracts.

The net gain up front from subtracting the $4,705 from the $7,760 amount is $3,055, minus any commissions. This $3,055 proves to be the optimal potential profit on the trade. You gain this entire amount if the expiration day silver futures prices on November 24th are located anywhere over $24.00.

The most that you could lose would be the difference between the two put strike price differences of $1.00 or $5,000 minus the credit that you received of $3,055, which equates to $1,945. This would be your situation if silver futures closed November 24th at any point below $23.00.

Naturally, you can vary your maximum losses and profit potentials by choosing varying strike prices. You might also widen or narrow the spread of the two strike prices to change these amounts. Once again, you are able to lock in some profits early should silver experience a significant move ahead of time.

Return to Table of Contents

Chapter 8

Powerful Silver Investment Strategies that Make You Money

"However beautiful the strategy, you should occasionally look at the results"

—ir Winston Churchill

In this chapter you learn various investment strategies that will provide you with the backbone to make the right decisions when you buy or sell. Buying and selling are the two things you must do to turn a profit. Besides that you will make a decision if you want to be a day trader, do short term trading or simple keep Silver until it has reached its peak point.

In simple terms you will learn when to buy low and when to sell high. That's basically all there is to know.

8.1 Keeping the Purity of a Single Solid Approach

By now you may be wondering which silver investment strategy is best for you. You have read about so many different vehicles for investing in silver that your head may be starting to spin. From buying physical silver bullion and silver coins, to purchasing silver ETF shares like SLV and AGQ, to obtaining numismatic coins and collectible coins, to opening an investment account with FOREX or COMEX, there really are a variety of different means and vehicles for investing in silver these days.

The best way to invest in silver is to find the means that you are the most comfortable with and confident in. Your silver investment vehicle should be one that you comprehend and about which you are not confused. There is no sense getting involved in a silver investment that you simply do not understand. This only leads to very real frustration and potential disappointment down the road.

If you are looking at several different silver investment opportunities and are not sure which one is the best for you personally, then you may be thinking that perhaps diversifying your silver investments is the best path to follow. The truth is that this is not the best way to purse investing in silver. In fact, you should only diversity your silver investment dollars if you do not know which one is right for you to get involved with personally.

There are a couple of reasons for this. On the one hand, if you have several different silver investments going, or even a number of different ones in which you are involved, then you will spend a great amount of time keeping up with them all. Having multiple accounts and silver investments may sound exciting and romantic, but it takes a lot of effort and concentration to manage them all.

Besides this, spreading your silver investment dollars around will cost you more money in commissions and fees. As an example, if you open a stock trading account with a discount broker such as TD Ameritrade or E-Trade, then you can place simple buy and sell orders on silver ETF shares for around $10 per order. This is the case whether you buy ten shares or ten thousand shares of a silver ETF.

The cost per trade is minute if you are trading large dollar amounts of silver. But if you instead buy only a few shares of several different ETFs, then you will pay the approximately $10 fee for each ETF entry and exit, doubling or even tripling your costs, depending on how many different ones that you diversity into at a time.

The same principal is true regarding choosing to buy a few silver bullion coins of one type, a few of another, and yet still more of a third kind. If instead you bought a 10 ounce or 100 ounce bullion coin or bar, then your per ounce premium on the silver would be 50 to 100 percent less.

Diversifying your silver investments will give you a big headache. It will also cost you in extra trading costs and fees. When each investment is basically geared to the same underlying basis of silver price per ounce, there is no need to do this. The only exception to this rule is when you simply can not make up your mind and settle on one type of silver investment.

8.2 Taxes for the Short and Long Terms

Another thing that you should consider in your silver investments is the tax impacts of various kinds of silver holdings. The two classes of investments for tax purposes are short term and long term holdings. The IRS treats each type differently for taxing purposes.

Long term investments are favored by the IRS's tax policy. A long term holding investment is considered to be one that is held by you the investor for more than one year. If you buy into a silver investment and keep it for at least the year and a day time frame, then you will be able to look forward to the lower capital gains tax rates when you sell it.

Capital Gains refers to the money that you make on the investment. It is determined by subtracting the buying price along with the commissions and fees from the selling price. The capital gains tax rates on such long term investments are either zero percent or 15 percent, depending on what your marginal tax bracket proves to be. If your marginal tax rate bracket is ten or 15 percent, then you will not pay any long term capital gains tax on your silver investment proceeds.

These rates are good through the end of 2010, when they will likely increase to at least 15 percent as a minimum. If you are a member of the twenty-three, twenty-eight, thirty-three, or 35 percent tax brackets, then you will pay the 15 percent long term capital gains tax rates.

If you instead trade in and out of silver investments more frequently, as in day trading or pattern trading, then your tax rate for the investment capital gains will be treated by the IRS as short term capital gains. Short term capital gains are those that you hold for a year or less. Such short term capital gains prove to be taxed at your typical income tax rate. This is still a relatively low rate if you are in the ten or 15 percent tax bracket, but it gets higher if you are in the 25, 28, 33, or 35 percent tax brackets.

Because of this, your silver investment strategy should be impacted by in which tax bracket you fall. Short term silver trading is fine and well if you benefit from the lower ten and 15 percent tax brackets, but it gets very expensive if you are taxed in the higher rate brackets. Long term silver trading proves to be less expensive no matter in which tax bracket you find yourself. Remember that your holding period is figured up from the point at which you purchase your silver investment to the point that you sell it. Keep this in mind as you are deciding how to pursue your silver investment strategy.

8.3 Buying Strategy 101 – On the Way Down

Use this trading strategy only when the silver price is in a zig zag pattern, which means it is going up for a certain time and then it is going down for a certain time.

This is a simple strategy to get more leverage on your future earnings. Let's say silver is at $20 and you bought 100 shares, equal to a $2,000 investment. When the price is going down you don't sell of course. You wait until the price goes up and higher than your original purchase price of $20. You wait to sell however long it takes for you to make a profit. You only start making a profit when the price passes $20 and you sell.

Let's assume the silver price goes down to $18 and you buy another 100 shares, or $1,800 worth. Now you have $3,800 invested in your portfolio of silver altogether and you have 200 shares. Your average purchase price of one share is now $19. What that simply means is that you do not have to wait as long to get back into the profit zone. Now you are in the profit zone when the Silver price passes the $19 mark. You are now using leverage.

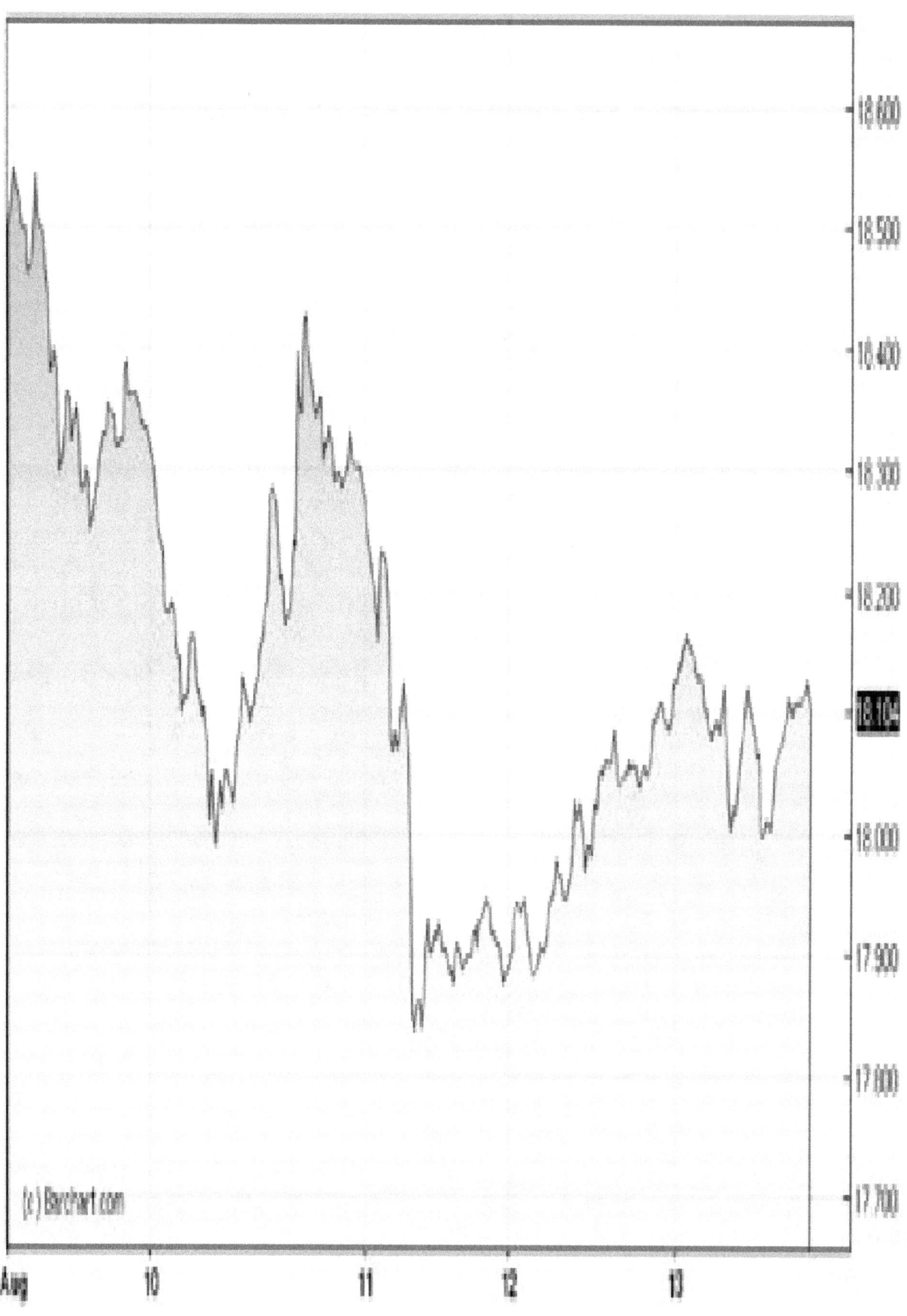

Above chart shows a 5 day trading range

You can do this trading pattern as long as the silver price is going down. Of course that's only possible if you were smart enough not to put all your money into one purchase contract.

When you first think about buying more when the price goes down it seems counter intuitive as you invest more on a falling price. But as I illustrated in the example, it is a great way to have your ducks in a row when the price starts to go up again, and that's just a matter of time.

8.4 Buying Strategy 102 – On the Way Up

Use this trading strategy only when the silver price is in a zig zag patterns, which means it is going up for a certain time and then it is going down for a certain time.

Now why would you sell when the price goes up? Simply, because you want to take out your profit slowly before the price starts going down again. Every time the price of silver goes up, you sell a portion of it, and you put your profit into the bank. That's no longer paper money – it's real money that you cash out.

Each time you sell off a portion of your investment in this scenario you minimize the risk when silver goes down below your profit line before you can cash in on it. Again, this strategy looks counter intuitive as well. Your common sense tells you to just wait until you hit the top and then sell. But you never know when the top will happen. It may have happened at a time when you weren't paying attention and by the following day, you've missed your opportunity.

Trading this way minimizes your risk, however, it takes tremendous discipline and self-control. Use your head and control your greed. Greed is a sure-fire way to lose big when you do investing. I have seen this over and over in myself, losing a lot of money in the beginning especially by being greedy. Controlling your emotions is one major task that you will learn during your early investment learning curve.

8.5 The Rule of 21 – Buying Beer and Silver

This price may be higher or lower when you read this. $24 gets you one share of Silver when you use the Exchange Traded Fund SLV. You can check out the current price by putting SLV into Google. Usually it comes up as a graph on the first position. Click on the graph and you will get automatically into the financial section of Google and see a bigger chart of the SLV ETF and some other values. If it is during NYSE trading time you can actually see the live price of Silver SLV going up and down.

All what you you have to do in order to buy one share of SLV is to open a trading account with one of the big trading companies:

- TdAmeritrade
- Scottrade
- Fidelity
- ETrade
- Schwab

There are several other companies, but I recommend you stick with one of the big ones above. If you do not have an account you can sign up for free. In order to get started you need to deposit some money in your trading account. After that, you can start buying ETFs like SLV or AGQ like regular shares.

8.5.1 Avoid The Early Morning Orientation Period

Don't buy right away when the NYSE market opens. The majority of traders usually wait until the market opens to make their move. Silver is traded around the clock each day and, when the market opens, you will sometimes see adjustments that look like big moves up or down. Wait at least 30 minutes until the market has cooled down a bit before you sell or buy.

After 30 minutes you are usually able to see a day pattern evolve that is stable as long as no major news that can impact the market comes out. Major news can and will break the price pattern up or down. However, the least you can do is to cover your risk a bit by waiting this first 30 minutes. I have begun to trade several times in the past before the 30 minute mark and, most of the time, it has turned out not to be a wise decision.

Often, when I broke ranks with my trading discipline, the price went rapidly up or down and, in the heat of the moment, I reacted by buying or selling quickly. Don't do it! Keep your fingers away from the keyboard and go do something else for half an hour. Force yourself to come back only when the market has passed the 30-minute mark.

8.6 Taming Calculated Risk 103

Another of the most powerful investment tools for your silver investments that you should work into your strategies revolves around using margin accounts and leverage. They way to significantly increase your profits with silver is through the judicious and effective use of such leverage, as we have discussed in the past chapters.

For example, when you control $10,000 worth of physical silver ounces, and silver prices rise five percent, then your investment gains $500 in value. This is a respectable gain, but it will not change your life.

If instead you are able to employ 2:1 leverage using a standard stock brokerage margin account, then your gains will be better. A $20,000 investment in a silver ETF will grow by $1,000 with a similar five percent rise in silver prices. But since you have only put up $10,000, your gains have been realized at a ten percent rate. Your investment has similarly grown at twice the dollar value with this amount of leverage.

With the greater leverage of 4:1 that can be obtained by buying the AGQ Pro Shares Ultimate Silver ETF in a margin account, your investment gains become still more impressive. An investment of $10,000 now controls $40,000 worth of exposure to silver. A five percent move in the underlying silver price is now making $2,000 increases in your investment. This amounts to 20 percent real gains on the $10,000 with which you started.

Even higher leverage of 15:1 can be obtained on silver investments using COMEX futures contracts. Once again, look at the numbers and you will start to appreciate how major leverage can make enormous differences in returns on silver holdings. With $10,000 you can control a substantial $150,000 worth of silver futures contracts at 15:1 margin. The same five percent return is now yielding a more impressive $7,500 gain in your silver investment. This amounts to a significant 75 percent return on your original $10,000 with which you began the investment.

Finally, the greatest margin leverage that you can get with silver investments is through FOREX foreign exchange held silver in the form of the XAG/USD, silver against the dollar. As mentioned in earlier chapters, the leverage with this type of silver holding is 25:1. Now the $10,000 used in all of the above examples is controlling $250,000 worth of a silver position.

The gains become staggering, as a five percent increase in silver prices translates to $12,500. You have now realized an increase in your position that is greater than your original investment amount of $10,000. The return at this rate amounts to 125 percent.

Leverage and margin accounts with silver investments can make all of the difference in the world. Imagine if the silver price gains are not simply five percent, but 20 percent over time. On a FOREX account $250,000 holding of XAG/USD, this turns into a $50,000 gain on just a $10,000 original investment. This is a staggering 500 percent return on investment. Now, that is an amount of money that can impact your wealth building and standard of living.

8.7 What Temperature Is Your Thermometer Reading Now?

Since you are going to be putting a potentially significant amount of your investment capital into silver for hoped for long term appreciation, you should understand a few of the factors that influence the price of silver on a routine basis. Three external factors typically impact silver prices. These revolve around the value of the dollar, how well the economy is doing, and the going interest rates.

Silver, like gold, often moves inversely in price and value to that of the U.S. dollar. This is not hard to understand, since silver and gold are both valued in terms of U.S. dollars as a standard procedure. As the dollar goes up, silver tends to fall in value. As the dollar falls, silver tends to rise in value.

One of the strongest arguments for silver lies in the increasing worries that the U.S. dollar has been overly valued considering how many new dollars have been created in the past few years. If you are a big believer in an eventually lower dollar, as has been the long term trend, then you will have little trouble understanding how higher silver prices are likely to result in the future.

Silver is different from gold in how it responds to the state of the economy. On the one hand, its investment appeal does lend it some support as a safe haven when the economic outlook darkens.

On the other hand, it is a heavily utilized industrial metal whose demand often falls when the economy slows significantly down. As you saw in an earlier chapter, in the Great Recession's main year of 2008, silver prices fell in the short term as the economy tanked. Silver prices tend to rise then when the world economic outlook remains solid, and to struggle when the economic output looks set to contract.

Interest rates similarly impact silver prices and values. Higher interest rates generally lead to higher silver prices. This is because higher interest rates commonly signal inflation and a battle against it. Inflation always pushes up silver and gold prices. Even the fear of inflation can lead to higher silver prices, as you have seen in the last several years of rampant money printing that has only supported and boosted the prices for both the yellow and gray metals.

Obviously, there are many internal factors that influence the value of silver prices. Supply and demand are the chief of these, as with most commodities in the world. Still, the three external factors discussed above do play a significant role in the short, medium, and long term movements in silver prices.

8.8 Kicking Out the House Guest

How long do you keep your silver investment? It all depends on the trading strategy you want to use. You can do short term trading, which means you buy and sell every few days, or go for long term trading, which means you may hold your silver until it has reached it's highest point. Besides these two trading strategies, you can also engage in day trading, which requires the most mathematical and financial intelligence of all three trading strategies.

Long Term Trading

This is the simplest form of investing in silver. You basically buy when you have some liquid money around and hold onto your buy for the next few years. As we are currently in a commodity bull market, you probably can't go wrong with this strategy. You also have a tax advantage. You will be taxed only 13 percent if you hold silver longer than a year. This is probably the least exciting method to make money with silver, but it is also the least risky. The strategy here is to profit from silver in the long run with the understanding that silver will go up for the next few years.

Short Term Trading

With short term trading you buy and sell silver more often. Perhaps you make one or two transactions per week. The strategy here is to profit from short term political trends. Every piece of news that comes out regarding decisions around currency and silver will lead to a price change. Every bit of news that involves the economy leads to a price change either large or small. The market is dynamic and open to information inflows and outflows from all sources, but especially ones that deal with money or the economy. The overall trend for silver is still rising, however, you will make additional money by using short price declines over the period of one, two, or three days.

Day Trading

The main difference between day trading silver with a FOREX or Futures and Commodities account involves the size of the contract amounts and leverage involved. FOREX trading of silver is done using the XAG/USD, or silver against the dollar currency pair. With FOREX accounts, you are able to trade as little as even 100 ounces of silver. This is nice as you are just getting started, as you can do real trades without putting a lot of money at risk. Every full dollar move in silver will only cost you or make you $100 like this. The FOREX accounts also allow for 25:1 margin.

Futures and Commodities accounts trading on the COMEX provides smaller margin but larger trade sizes. 15:1 is offered by the silver contracts. Full-size contracts are for 5,000 ounces of silver. Full-size contracts make or lose $25 per contract with every five cent move in the silver price. Mini-account contracts are for 1,000 ounces of silver. With silver mini contracts, one cent moves translate to a more manageable $1 per contract gain or loss.

Day trading with silver involves buying and selling some form of silver one or more times in a single day. True day trading never seeks to hold the silver position overnight, but instead purchases it and sells it all in the same trading day. This type of trading involves trading the metal mostly using technical indicators. Technical trading involves following a number of different charts and patterns to know at what point to buy and at what point to sell. A few of the more popular technical indicators used to day trade silver are explained for you below.

The most important elements to successfully day trading silver are to utilize a strategy with great discipline and to work with a fast trading plan. You will need a good and quick plan for day trading silver markets. The easy part is looking at daily and weekly charts to figure out a general overall direction of silver. The discipline portion of successful day trading silver is more difficult. Unless you follow a strategy with discipline, then you will not succeed.

The majority of silver day traders are simply technical traders. This means that they look at short term and long term price movements of silver in order to predict upcoming movements in price. You should master this if you want to day trade. You should also know silver's basic fundamentals, including supply and demand and the impact of relevant markets like gold. Having this wider lens on the market will assist you in figuring out your best buy and sell prices, as well as in understanding what the price charts are telling you about oversold or overbought scenarios.

A few of the most heavily utilized technical indicators are highlighted below, as follows:

• Moving Averages are the average silver prices for a certain period of time.

• Stochastic is a measurement that helps to know which direction the momentum is going.

• Relative Strength Index (RSI) tracks how powerfully the silver markets are going in a certain up or down direction. This is mostly utilized to determine if the silver market is oversold or overbought.

• Moving Average Convergence-Divergence (MACD) proves to be one indicator that merges a number of moving averages' data

To start out with day trading, you will want to have a daily chart that helps you to determine what the short term trend is. This will guide you on whether you ought to buy silver when the price pulls back, or sell it when it is rallying. When the daily chart shows a short term trend that has been falling, then you ought to be more likely to sell any rally at a resistance point. Significant resistances on day trades are located on a 60 minute time frame chart where the old support was found, or alternatively at prices that were high points in the market previously.

Then, you should look at a bar chart that is shown in a 10 minute time frame. Doing so will assist you in figuring out if the appropriate price levels prove to be practical trade entry points for the day trade. After you have decided what the best entry price is, then you have to move on to determining your price movement goal as well as your strategy for exiting the trade.

Before you get into a silver day trade, you have to know how much the trade will put at risk. To do this, simply find the next resistance point in case the one you are selling against does not hold. If you were looking to buy silver on a pullback, you would look for the next support level in case the first one did not hold up. Figuring out your profit goal is also a matter of looking for the next support or resistance levels. It is important to not put more at risk then you are looking to make on the trade, in order to be successful over the short and longer term.

You actually enter your trade, regardless of whether you are buying or selling silver, as the price approaches the level you are watching and the MACD indicator crosses to show a sell or buy signal on a ten minute chart. Once the MACD has given the go ahead sign, then you can enter your trade and set up your take profit and limit loss points.

As you can see silver day trading requires the most financial know how. I would only suggest this option if you are already an advanced trader and understand technical analysis. If you are new to silver trading please stay away from this option, even you can make the most money in the shortest time period.

8.9 Know When to Exit

Every investment has its entry and its exit. At one point your investment will no longer throw off any money or go up in its value. With silver in particular, there will come a time when the value of the metal drops, the long term trend reverses, and silver goes down in price.

That will probably happen after the dollar has either crashed or becomes massively devalued by hyperinflation. At this point in time gold and silver will revaluate to the most stable currency that is either on the market or will be pegged to a new index of some sort in terms of value. Watch out when interest rates begin going up again. This will be a sure indicator that silver will drop, if not permanently at least for the time.

Return to Table of Contents

Chapter 9

The Next Ten Years - Predictions for the Global Economy

"I have seen the future and it is very much like the present, only longer."

—Kehlog Albran

Nothing stays the same – everything changes. Change itself the only constant. Sometimes we see fewer changes, sometimes more. Right now we are in a time frame with major changes. Changes that are going so fast that we hardly can keep up with it.

I personally attribute these changes to evolutionary cycles. Humanity has developed many ways of thinking about and preparing for cycles of change. If you want to know more about this topic you may find it interesting to study the Mayan calendar, which frames vast cycles of time and chronicles change in terms of human evolution.

During these days of sensationalized news, whatever you may have heard about the Mayan calendar is mostly wrong. The world will not end in 2012, however, that year does designate the end of a billion year cycle and the beginning of the next billion year cycle. Certainly within the lifespan of a single human being, change in a universal sense will not be so dramatic. We nevertheless feel change in our lives and the overall tenor of this change is tempered and influenced by the larger cycle. There is nothing to worry about as long as we are willing to adapt and change.

With that said let's look what the next ten years may bring. Of course, nobody knows the future. However, when you have enough data from the past and you know a bit about human behavior you can make predictions – and that's what I will try to accomplish in this chapter.

It will get rough for a while before it gets better. A better financial system will be put in place that is based on a quite different way to look at how we negotiate for goods and services with our medium of exchange. At one point in the future, our current medium of exchange may no longer be needed. Imagine a world in which money per se does not exist!

I personally look forward to this time. Money is, after all, just an invention like inches or seconds, a tool that only takes us so far. It may have outlived its usefulness already and in the future, perhaps there will come a time when human beings find ways to do business with each other, build up and protect their material security, and offer value to others in ways that go beyond money. I firmly believe that all we really need are material resources and creativity. Money is actually just a byproduct of these two things.

9.1 Sturm und Drang – The Thunder of the Next Ten Years

You may be wondering what the economic outlook for the next decade will be. There are many economists telling you that things will continue to stabilize and improve within that time frame. These are the same economists who never saw the Great Recession coming.

From that select few economists who did successfully present in advance the coming housing crash and ensuing economic turmoil, you hear a far less rosy prognosis on the economic future. A book that you may have heard of came out at the beginning of 2006 called America's Bubble Economy.

Authors David Wiedemer, Robert Wiedemer, and Cindy Spitzer correctly foretold the popping of a variety of bubbles that practically no one saw coming. These were the housing bubble, private debt bubble, stock market bubble, and consumer spending bubble that resulted in so much economic pain and misery. Unfortunately for the next ten years, these economists who saw the previous crash coming before hand say that the worst is not over.

Their new book Aftershock talks about what they see coming over the next decade. Just as most economists missed the prior crash, they are similarly not paying attention to the fundamental problems that are still with the system and are only getting worse.

Rather than things returning to the way they were before the Great Recession, they will only continue to deteriorate. Two more larger bubbles have yet to pop, and these will begin to do so in the next several years. These are the bubbles of the federal government debt and the U.S. dollar.

The reason that this economic malaise will only continue and worsen is because what is actually occurring is that a multiple bubble economy that was built up over more than twenty years, centered in the United States, is now popping and coming undone.

The first phase of it that occurred in 2006-2008 proved to be bad, but these economist authors see the next phase of it being considerably more dangerous. In the coming years, those who hold on to the wealth and capital that they have will be extremely fortunate. Those who make money will be extremely rare.

This means that the economic outlook over the next ten years will be bleak. Rather than growing economies and easing of credit conditions that you have heard about from the same talking heads who turned out to be clueless before, you will instead see temporary recoveries followed by even worse economic collapses. There are a number of reasons for this to be the case.

The problems in the system have not been fixed. First, the bubbles were built up using cheap and easy money and credit that was facilitated by the Federal Reserve with low interest rates over prolonged periods of time. Second, regulations were removed, such as the Glass-Steagall Act, that allowed financial weapons of mass destruction to be created.

Finally, banks were allowed to lawlessly invest their own money and effectively that of their stake holders and depositors in a casino-style environment where they put far more at risk than they could cover in a significant downturn. These problems are all still with us, as they have not been addressed, but only wall papered over.

Instead of pursuing a more sound long term interest rate policy, the Fed has responded to the economic crisis by cutting rates to their lowest historic levels for an extended period. In so doing, they hope to make money and credit cheap and easy again. Their goal that you see them pursuing is to essentially re-inflate the bubbles that were popped so violently over the last three to four years.

They will be unsuccessful at this because such bubbles can not be re-inflated after they have popped. The mask has been removed, and the artificial run up in real estate and all that was based on it has been effectively exposed. People will certainly think twice before falling for that bubble again soon.

The removal of regulations over the last 20 plus years has also facilitated banks making irresponsible loans and creating investments that were complicated and dangerous. Sub prime mortgages may now be a thing of the past, but the investments that banks packaged up and created using them are not.

These CDOs, or collateralized debt obligations, are still festering in the system, existing in the trillions of dollars, as they did before the crash and still do. The worst part of it is that the banks did not learn from the disaster of the real estate collapse and are still busy re-packaging such loans in great numbers like in 2006. This is another disaster that will continue to harm the economy going forward.

Finally, banks are still risking both their own and their stake holders' and depositors' money by being involved with complicated and dangerous investments like credit default swaps. These expose them all to one bank's failure through a complicated interconnected web.

Rather than the governments of the world stepping in to break up this off accounting sheet market that totals in the tens of trillions of dollars, they have instead offered incentives for the banks to bring these complex transactions on to their balance sheets. As a result, the credit default swaps have continued to grow, and still present another looming threat to the worldwide financial system over the coming few years.

9.2 The Fat Lady Isn't About to Sing Yet

Another reason that things will never simply go back to the way that they were before the Great Recession and financial meltdown is that this did not prove to be a typical recession with a definite starting point and ending date. Instead, what you saw happen to the U.S. and world economy was the beginning of a transition.

One old economic system fell into irreversible decline, and another one will take shape from the final ruin. The U.S. economy is ceasing to be the bedrock of the world economy that it has been since the end of World War II, and the dollar is being phased out as the world's reserve currency that it has been since the Breton Woods Agreement.

This is where the continuing popping of the remaining two bubbles of the U.S. Federal government debt and the U.S. dollar come into play. In the next few years, you will see the Federal government debt shell game finally come to a dramatic and unpleasant end. Investors around the world will start to wake up to the fact that they will never actually be repaid by the largest Ponzi scheme in the history of the world.

Once government debt holders realize that they are only being paid back their earlier money by new investor money, and that the government can never hope to repay all of its out of control debt, the foreign investors who so faithfully support the U.S. debt will flee for the exits.

In the process, you will see the government have its credit card cut and its interest rates massively raised. Once this occurs, the government will be unable to pay the interest on the debt and keep up with its other many obligations to its citizens. Incapable of living off of its tax revenue base as it will then have to, the government will be forced to decide between massively cutting back on domestic and military expenditures or paying interest and principal payments on the debt at the new and significantly higher rate of interest.

They will inevitably choose to default on the debt rather than face the wrath of citizens who will have otherwise had all of the promises that were made to them by the government completely broken. At that point, government debt will be exposed for what it has always been, worthless paper.

Meanwhile, much of the economy will have been badly harmed in the process. Part of this will result from the subsequent fall of the dollar bubble along with the government debt bubble. As the trillions of dollars of foreign held government debt is liquidated and repatriated, the supply of dollars offered on the market will be simply too great for international demand to absorb.

This will cause a sudden and precipitous fall of the artificially inflated dollar bubble at a shocking pace. Between the two remaining bubbles bursting, any hope of a sustained economic recovery happening will be promptly squashed. The transition to a newer and eventually more stable economic system for the world will be well underway at this point.

For all of these reasons, it is safe to say that this is not your usual recession that you have seen several times in the past few decades. It is the end of an economic system. Because of this, all of the pain and dislocation presently associated with it are far from over today. The next few years will be very bumpy, so brace yourself by making preparations before it is too late.

9.3 Nero Said Everything Was Just Peachy

The problem with listening to the government about the economic outlook for the coming years is that they have a long and established track record of only telling the people what they want to hear. This is in their best interest of making sure that the population remains both upbeat and in line.

Unfortunately, since the government officials are mostly elected, their reelections are often based in large part on expressing a rosier outlook for the economy than the real facts on the ground convey. Most Americans will still accept what their government officials like the President and Chairman of the Federal Reserve tell them at face value. The truth is that these self same officials commonly lie to you, telling you that everything is fine about the economy while in reality it is not.

Examples of this abound. For the first months of the Great Recession, Chairman of the Federal Reserve Ben Bernake continued to claim that a minor setback in the economy was underway. Housing prices would correct a little, but the dangers to the economy were limited in scale and scope, he insisted.

Even when the evidence piled up heavily to the contrary, he continued downplaying the severity of the contraction and underlying economic problems. Even years after the fact, most Americans are only dimly aware that the banking system nearly collapsed on a weekend in October of 2008. Yet at the time, Treasury Secretary Henry Paulson gave repeated interviews assuring that everything was fine and the government was on top of the situation.

Take the measurements of economic performance as another example. Over a long term span of thirty years, politicians in Washington applied continuous pressure to the Federal economists in order to make them alter the ways that they analyze important measurements of the national economy. This has been done deliberately to make the economic numbers look better than they really are, so that the politicians in power could be protected from voters who would be very angry if they knew how bad things really were getting.

The unemployment rate is the most obvious example. Under President Clinton, the official formula used for figuring it was changed. It resulted in lower unemployment numbers from that point forward, in particular when a major crisis in the economy occurs. Consider that with an official unemployment rate of 9.7 percent, the actual number of discouraged workers and part time employees who want full time employment should really be a crushing 21.6 percent, on a level comparable with that of the Great Depression.

The formula for inflation has also been tinkered with to produce a lower CPI number. This has been done by conveniently changing the components' weightings with time, supposedly to reflect a more accurate reality. With a 2.1 percent CPI inflation level, the actual inflation is really closer to 5.5 percent.

Another example of the government lying to you about the economy and or conveniently hiding the truth is found in the Federal Reserve's decision to stop reporting M3 back in the late 1980's. M3 proved to be the broadest and most accurate depiction of the money supply. It also exposed whenever the government increased the money supply, and kept them from hiding their cheapening of the currency over time. To keep the truth from you about how they were literally printing away the value of the dollar, they simply stopped disclosing it.

You must remember that the government is vested in keeping the voters happy and the system going. Because of this, they will not admit to how bad things really are when they are actually bad. Learn to research real economic performance for yourself, and you will not be an ignorant prisoner of the optimistic exaggerations any longer.

9.4 A Casket for a Currency

In the next ten years, you are going to look back and realize that the Great Recession actually marked the beginning of the end of the present financial system and dollar hegemony that has existed in the world since the Second World War.

This will be brought about by the sudden loss of confidence in the U.S. led world economy. When the government debt bubble finally pops, the stage will be fully set for the dollar to drop rapidly and drastically. You may be wondering how the dollar came to be in a bubble in the first place.

The bubble in the dollar came about as a result of President Nixon ending the U.S. dollar alignment to the gold standard back in 1971. Until that point, the dollar contained an intrinsic value that was equivalent to a certain amount of gold kept in government vaults. This provided the dollar with great stability year in and year out.

When the United States abandoned the gold standard, the dollar instantly lost all of its intrinsic value and entered a multiple decade bear market from which it has never recovered nor escaped. The end result of this has been a consistent and long term erosion of the dollar's value, interspersed by periodic bear market rallies. As these bear market rallies took place, it was easy for you and most Americans to forget that a bear market in the dollar continued to rage.

You might even have become convinced that the dollar is a safe haven in the meanwhile. This is an all too common false perception, since the rallies in the bear market of the dollar calmed down investors to the point that they were blindsided every time as the bear market in the greenback resumed. Finally, this bear market in the dollar will reach its epic low as the majority of Americans and even foreign investors have become the victims of intense losses on all assets that are denominated in dollars. This means that U.S. stocks, bonds, real estate, Treasuries, and CDs will all suffer the same fate at that time, since they are all investments whose values are related in terms of dollars.

Along with the end of the dollar as a reserve currency will come the end of the present financial system. This event will be far reaching in its impacts and effects. As oil, gold, silver, and other commodities are no longer priced in dollars at that point, the affordability of these essential commodities will skyrocket for all Americans.

Banks and Central Banks will dump their dollar reserves for some other currency that will have to arise to replace the dollar. Right now, the only contenders for this position of alternative reserve currency are either the euro or gold and silver.

Naturally, the end of the dollar as the world's reserve currency will entail a great amount of pain and loss of wealth for the typical American. Imports, including energy, will become horrifically expensive as the dollar resets to a far lower value. Foreign travel will likely once more become a luxury of the wealthy, as it was in times past. The dislocation in the U.S. economy will cause many industries to contract substantially, leading to an unemployment rate that will likely make today's near ten percent unemployment look respectable.

Foreign countries will also be dramatically impacted by the end of the present financial system and dollar. Those whose economies are heavily based on exports, particularly to the U.S., will also be in a great deal of trouble. This includes Germany and Japan principally. Those with large holdings of U.S. Dollars and dollar denominated debt will also suffer severe setbacks. This includes China and most of the oil rich Arab sultanates of the Middle East. Their enormous and impressive stock piles of U.S. treasuries at that point will be kindling for fire wood.

It is obvious that this change to a new financial system and world reserve currency will be difficult. Even though the American people will bear the brunt of the adjustment, foreigners will similarly suffer in the upheaval. This is particularly the case for those countries that are tied most closely to the U.S. economy, trade, and economic system.

9.5 Please Mister, Can You Spare a Hundred Bucks?

All of these monumental changes that are already in motion in the world economy and financial system will actually transpire over the next five years. In that time span, you will see the U.S. government debt scheme fail and the U.S. dollar purchasing power go to pieces. When this happens, you can count on the U.S. government attempting to print its way out of the crisis initially. It will come down to a choice of this or not paying the bills for domestic spending like Medicare and Social Security.

Over the last few years, the government has already demonstrated its ability and willingness to majorly increase the money supply in an attempt to restore the falling economy and to pay for stimulus. They have done this to the tune of a 300 percent increase to the total U.S. dollar base money supply around the world.

Imagine how much farther they will be willing to go with the electronic printing press when things get really bad, for example when the proverbial U.S. treasury bill unlimited spending credit card is rejected by the foreign investors.

If the U.S. no longer has anyone to buy its debt and loan it money, then it will be left with the other alternative of simply printing more money to cover the increasing shortfalls.

While the government can and does simply print extra money to pay the bills and for spending, there is a consequence for engaging in these actions, particularly when they start increasing the number of available dollars exponentially.

Inflation is always the product of too many paper bills chasing too few goods and services; this is why it is called a currency driven event. You have not yet seen the effects and results of these actions from the last round of money printing that went on in the last few years.

When the government attempts to create really enormous quantities of lower valued dollars to pay for things, then you will see hyperinflation of the currency. Hyperinflation is typically in the hundreds of percent per year, though it can reach hundreds and even thousands of percent per month as governments resort increasingly to printing more and more money in a vain attempt to solve their problems. You may say that hyperinflation could never happen in the United States, but the truth is that it already has on three separate occasions.

During the Revolutionary War, the new American government saw its continental dollars succumb to the ravages of hyperinflation as they printed too many of them to pay for the war. In the Civil War, hyperinflation also reared its ugly head, particularly in the Confederacy of the South. President Franklin Roosevelt also invited hyperinflation in 1933 when he devalued the dollar by 50 percent against gold. In some instances of hyperinflation in places like post World War I Germany, paper money has become so worthless that a wheelbarrow of it is necessary to purchase a single loaf of bread.

Hyperinflation causes many terrible effects for a nation and its people. Not the least of them is the encouragement to spend all money as soon as it is earned and received, since it will be worth less the next day.

Savers are ruined by hyperinflation, particularly those who are stuck on fixed incomes, such as retirees. Economic activity also suffers badly for lack of price and wage stability within the economy and an uncertain future outlook. Jobs are lost as part of the effects, and many important goods become unaffordable for many people.

Hyperinflation does not go on forever. When the government that is responsible for it begins raising interest rates and stops printing money, it settles down and an economy gradually returns to normal. Unfortunately, many people are ruined by such hyperinflation before it is brought back under control.

The good news is that one of the few investments that does not suffer from hyperinflation actually thrives in it. This is silver and gold. Precious metals are your ultimate protection against the coming instability and hyperinflation of the next few years. Once it starts, their present values will appear astonishingly cheap.

9.6 Leveling the Unlevel Playing Field with a World-wide Solution

In the last few years since the beginning of the global financial crisis, you have already seen a number of proponents calling for a new global currency to replace the dollar. The Chinese and some Middle Eastern nations have been at the vanguard of this movement that has for now been put down.

As a result of this sudden and calamitous fall of the dollar that is coming, these cries will no longer be able be able to suppressed any more as they were in the aftermath of the so called U.S. mismanaged global economy.

When all faith has been lost in the dollar as a result of the collapse of the U.S. government debt and resulting dollar crash and burn, a new global currency will not only be necessary, it will be demanded by an overwhelming majority of numerous influential countries around the world. Economists have speculated for several years what this new currency will look like.

Some have suggested that the euro will be the next currency to replace the dollar as the global reserve currency. The problem with this is that it is only another currency that can be manipulated by a single group who controls it.

The Euro Group nations and their board and president, along with their European Central Bank, have the ability to print more of the Euro, to boost its value through intervention, or to encourage its decline as it suits them. In the end, this would not make it a much better choice than the U.S. dollar, apart from the hesitance of its governing bodies and institutions to interfere with it too much.

Others have instead voiced support for an IMF unit of currency, which would be based on a so called basket of currencies. This would eliminate the problem of one nation or group being able to dictate its value to every one else. Still, a currency whose components are constantly changed to reflect growing and shrinking national economic influence would lack the stability and permanence that the new world currency will need to have.

Gold may be a part of the new currency, or serve as a bridge to the new currency, after the dollar's role as the world's reserve currency has been finished. Still, there are many critics of going back to the gold standard who argue that a currency based on a commodity that is limited in quantity would be too restrictive. Increasing the money supply using a gold backed currency means increasing the amount of available gold reserves.

What you will eventually see will be a truly international currency that is not based on any single or even basket of currencies. For this to happen, an agency like the International Monetary Fund will have to become the central banker to the world. Some would argue that it has been gradually assuming this role and accompanying powers, especially in light of the U.S. led worldwide financial meltdown.

A global currency will be needed to facilitate trade between borders. Currently, the vast majority of international trade via imports and exports are settled in U.S. dollars. It is necessary for all parties to have a single medium of exchange in which they can complete their transactions, so that they are not having to reconcile the differences between two different currencies at every stage of the transaction.

A truly global currency will more easily allow for such importing and exporting exchanges to go forward. Its value will not be constantly rising and falling. And a responsible institution like the IMF will be the one managing it and making sure that it is not over printed or inflated away to suit any petty national agendas.

You may look at the world today and say that there is no way that independent countries will surrender their sovereignty to the point of not having their own currency any longer. The enduring example of the European Union and single euro currency is proof that it is possible and can in fact happen when people grow tired enough of strife and economic instability.

After the more severe economic fallout from the downfall of the U.S. government debt and dollar bubbles, people will no longer cling to the sovereignty argument any longer, since they will be far more concerned with easing the pain and disruptive transition to the new economic system and currency.

9.7 Bye Bye White Picket Fence

Perhaps the most tragic victims of these tumultuous and turbulent economic shifts will prove to be the middle class. It is a sure thing that they will ruined by the fall of the dollar and the accompanying hyperinflation that results. There are a variety of reasons why this will turn out to be true.

The poor are already without much in the way of assets and value to lose. They exist on a day to day basis, living from paycheck to paycheck. As such their situation can worsen, but not so much. They have little to no retirement assets to lose. They do not own houses whose values can plummet with that of the overall economy.

They certainly do not have stocks, bonds, and other investments that are sensitive to the performance of the economy and can therefore dramatically decline. These people are already in the lowest echelon of society, and as such, they have no lower to fall. There will certainly be a far greater number of the poor after these events transpire than there are now.

The rich learn how to protect themselves from disaster and economic collapse as part of their financial training. You may have heard the saying before that the difference between the wealthy and the rest of us is that wherever they are, the rich always know where the back door can be found. This is certainly the case with their investments. Most any wealthy person has already hedged against a possible economic collapse by owning gold and silver as part of their asset holdings.

They often have foreign currency stashed away in Swiss Bank accounts or other offshore bank accounts overseas as well. While their stocks, bonds, and real estate investments would likely suffer as badly as the middle class' holdings would, falling to shockingly low levels with their real value dollar decline, the breathtaking increases in the values of their precious metals and foreign currencies will dramatically offset their other investment declines, leaving them still wealthy.

Alas, most members of the middle class do not have such vital protection in place. They have been fed the logic by the media and investment adviser elites that the smartest place to have their retirement and other investment monies are in stocks, bonds, and mutual funds. These same groups have cautioned the middle class against complicated foreign investments like currencies, and the so called risks associated with silver and gold holdings.

As a result of this bad advice that they have been given concerning protecting themselves, the vast majority of the middle class have little to no exposure to either foreign currencies or precious metals. Instead, their assets are almost entirely denominated in U.S. dollars.

So when the dollar plummets to a fraction of its present value, the value of their assets will plunge and never recover. On top of this tragic series of events, many in the middle class will lose their jobs and livelihoods as a part of the economic disruption and dislocation brought on by government defaulting on its debt, severe currency devaluation, and hyperinflation's insidious effects.

The saddest part of the ruin of the middle class will be that it proved to be completely unnecessary. If someone had only bothered to tell these people about the critical role that hard assets such as silver and gold should play in backing up any investment portfolio and providing true protection and diversification, then they might have obtained some silver and gold bullion.

Since the overwhelming majority of the middle class do not have this most essential of financial insurance as part of their strategies, they will be caught up and overwhelmed in the continuing and increasingly severe economic storm of the next ten years.

The economic outlook for the next ten years is not so optimistic as you hear about on the news every night. Still, once the present economic system is replaced by a newer and better one, things will stabilize and improve over time. The challenge simply lies in getting through the turbulent time in between the fall of the present economic system and the rise of the new one.

With investments in silver, you can be one of the few people who does this successfully.

Yours truly

Thomas Herold

Investor and Financial Educator

Bonus Wealth Building Course

From Financial Ignorance to Building Wealth in the Next 90 Days

As a free bonus for purchasing this book you are entitled for a free membership to the Wealth Building Course. This course is currently in development and will be completed in the first or second quarter of 2011.

The regular purchase price for this complete financial education course will be $998 once it is completed and released. As an early subscriber you receive the entire course for free.

It is structured into 12 weekly lessons and it covers all aspects of creating wealth for yourself and others. As you have come to understand from reading this book, money as currency comes and goes and fluctuates around government policy. Wealth is the real deal as it has intrinsic value. Wealth is the assets that generate money for you.

Please click on the following link to sign up and get your free course membership: http://www.wealthbuildingcourse.com

Stay Updated With The Latest Silver Trends

In your quest for a good, ongoing financial education you will find that there are not too many free information sources of value available, even on the Internet. The following two are my personal favorites and provide fantastic information about gold and silver that, on other major financial websites, are very costly.

Jim Sinclair – JSMineset.com

One such invaluable source for keeping on top of events going on in the world that affect the values of your stocks, bonds, and gold and silver investments is JSmineset.com.

The purveyor of this extremely helpful informational website is the legendary gold and silver adviser and investor Jim Sinclair.

Jim Sinclair is an interesting expert on precious metals of whom it is said that he has already forgotten more about gold than most of you ever knew about it. He is principally a specialist in the precious metals and a trader of commodities and foreign currencies.

Back in 1977, he established his Sinclair Group of Companies that provided customers with a full range of brokerage services covering stocks, bonds, and a variety of other types of investments. His companies had branches located in New York, Chicago, Kansas City, Toronto, Geneva, and London. He sold these companies in 1983.

As he was running these companies and following their sale, Jim Sinclair served as the precious metals adviser to the Hunt family and Hunt Oil in liquidating their massive silver position that they had built up in an attempt to corner the limited silver market. The Hunt Brothers had acquired enormous amounts of futures contracts on silver that gave them the right to buy physical silver at a certain set price.

In controlling increasingly larger silver positions, they were successful in drastically driving up the prices of silver to an amazing high of $42 per share. The regulators stepped in and ordered them to unwind their positions. Jim Sinclair was instrumental in assisting them to do this, and in helping to negotiate a $1 billion loan that Paul Volcker, then Chairman of the Federal Reserve Board, arranged to help them in their efforts to close out the silver positions.

Jim has also been an executive committee member and General partner of two firms on the New York Stock Exchange. He has additionally served as President of a commodities clearing firm Sinclair Global Clearing Corporation as well as President of a dealer in currencies and metals, Global Arbitrage. Since then, Jim Sinclair has been involved as Chairman of Tanzanian Royalty Exploration, heading up its endeavors to transform itself into a gold royalty company.

The legendary gold and silver dealer and investor has written three books and a great number of magazine articles. These cover the investment subjects of strategies for trading, acquiring precious metals, and geopolitical events as they pertain to the markets and economics of the world. As a regular and hugely popular speaker at gold conferences and events, his commentary on financial issues and especially gold receives widespread media coverage in the United States and around the world.

His website has a mission of being a teaching forum that is service oriented. They use the everyday markets for the backdrop of their texts and as their classroom blackboard. Jim Sinclair and three other contributors provide commentary that is intended to teach you a lesson about the mistakes being made by the world's policy makers that are affecting you and your money and investments. It is a proactive website that counsels you how to invest to protect yourself from the troubles that are ensuing from the world leaders' tragic mistakes.

Besides Jim Sinclair, the purveyor of the website, there are three other regular contributors. These men have specialties in different areas of investments and advising. Dan Norcini proves to be a professional on floor trader of commodities.

He contributes charting performed through technical analysis covering gold and silver bullion, crude oil and copper prices, the American dollar, the Canadian dollar, and the euro. Monty Guild is a contributor who runs an investment management services company that helps advise American and foreign investors and foreign and domestic investment firms.

Finally, David Duval turns out to be an internationally known author on the specialty of mining and minerals. As co-founder of JSmineset.com, he is managing editor when he is not acting as a consultant on minerals and technical adviser to the United Nations.

This enormously popular web site informational service has much to offer you. Each and every day, they post twenty-four hour charts in the upper left hand corner covering the prices of gold bullion, the U.S. dollar index, and the euro. They then re-print articles from a wealth of sources from literally around the world covering every bit of news related to the financial crisis, the inflationary printing of money, the state of the U.S. and other major economies, and other geopolitical concerns that have tremendous impact on your investments.

They similarly offer brief commentary on and lessons to be learned from these articles. From time to time, they write their own articles about events going on in the political and financial worlds and how they affect the prices of gold and other commodities and investments. You will not find a comparable site offering such a wealth of time saving and valuable information, and all at no charge, anywhere else on the Internet.

The website was partially founded as Jim Sinclair and the other contributors became concerned about a coming financial collapse that they began predicting way back in 2003. They saw that complicated financial instruments, called derivatives, had been created based on inflated real estate prices and bundled up risky home loans.

As the dollar amounts of these shadowy and unregulated investments began to grow into the trillions and then tens of trillions this past decade, Jim and the contributors referred to these derivatives as financial weapons of mass destruction that would blow the western based world economy to pieces one day.

They predicted that when this began to happen, that the price of gold would rise to $1,225, $1,250, then $1,650 an ounce, and all by or before 2011. Jim came up with a formula that he posted in September of 2006 to explain how it would all come to pass. When he made these astonishing predictions, gold prices were in the $500-$600 per ounce range. Gold drove to literally $1,225 per ounce on its first thrust above $1,200 before pulling back, as Jim Sinclair suggested that it would. It has since surged past $1,250 and is now on its way to $1,300.

Since gold has moved so quickly, and the U.S. and other countries have begun to print money at rates that are unprecedented by the leading economies in recent decades, he has since revised his predictions for gold prices to surpass $1,650, potentially going to as high as $5,000 per ounce in the coming years.

And what is true for gold is even more true for silver. We may see a silver price of $30 as soon as by the end of January 2011. If not by early 2011 then this will happen during or by the end of 2011.

To get the latest news automatically sign up at his website:
http://www.JSmineset.com

Michael Maloney – goldsilver.com and wealthcycles.com

Michael Maloney has been an entrepreneur since he turned seventeen years old. In his years as an entrepreneur, his goal morphed into one of being a worthy steward of the financial trust his family had placed in him. Because of this, Maloney began studying the economy of the world and the United States, as well as the financial markets. What he uncovered may surprise you to hear.

Michael Maloney learned that identical economic patterns repeated themselves again and again in history, starting back in the Ancient World and continuing to our own time. Literally each time that the currency of a state grew over inflated, it became devalued. Then the citizens understood that a journey back to silver and gold as the safe haven money proved to be essential for survival.

Maloney understood that what you see going on nowadays has occurred time and time again. His greatest revelation turned out to be that this same pattern is about to transpire once more. This time it will be far more intense than in the past, to the tune of several multiples greater.

Because of this understanding, Michael Maloney became convinced that in order to grow and safe guard the wealth of his family, he would need to buy into silver and gold. In time, Maloney opened a wildly successful silver and gold dealership. He wanted to do more than just buy into the precious metals. His goal lay in working with the naturally occurring economic cycles to do this. After years of research and study, he realized his dream to begin helping others to understand the economic and wealth building cycles of the market. This led to his writing the Guide to Investing in Gold and Silver that has already been read by tens of thousands of individuals.

It took Michael Maloney countless years as an entrepreneur, business owner, inventor, and even author to reach the point of starting up his dream company. WealthCycles.com is the product of the overwhelming demand of people like you in need of useful facts and practical financial guidance that they can use in their everyday lives to grow and protect their own wealth.

The WealthCycles.com is actually a resources website for financial education. It provides you with an all inclusive kit of tools of information that comprises historical viewpoints and pragmatic approaches to applications, as well as explanations for present day economic situations, helping individuals to find the ability to save their families, as well as to prosper and to secure their families' futures in the wake of the coming worldwide economic instabilities.

At this site, Maloney and company offer you easy to understand guidance for getting through the challenging financial system of today. In the process, they seek to stimulate your mind, entertain you, and motivate you as well. The site promises to help you through the most exciting opportunities for building up wealth that history has to offer, which Maloney and WealthCycles.com insist are just around the corner.

The site has a stated goal of helping you to learn all about the economics of wealth cycles so that you can take care of yourself and your family in the future. WealthCycles.com has been created to provide comprehensible and timely information pertaining to the economic cycles of wealth. As such, the site and company realize that information is becoming more and more important to your life in this age. Because so much information has become available, it is almost overwhelming to go through it and sift it for value and truth.

Although there are countless resources available online, alongside the twenty-four hour news cycle of both television and radio, WealthCycle.com knows that this proves to be far more financial information than you can possibly absorb. Besides this, far too much of the financial information on offer proves to be no more than propaganda or statistical noise. Much of this exists to frighten you rather than to help you learn.

Because of this, too many people are confused and bewildered by all of the data firing at them. You may feel the same way. One sided conversations and points of view are quoted out of and without the proper context on a seemingly daily basis.

Helping you to become both financially educated and a well informed person of what is really happening is part of this goal. The site and company see the need for a site to help people sift through the noise to get the most timely and correct financial information into your hands and lives in time to help you.

This means that their website concerns both educating you and teaching you to take critical and timely actions. First, you will have to understand what to do, so that you can take the necessary actions. To help you with this, they will show you the historical past and how it explains the future. They will combine the historical view with practical and present day analysis. Finally, they will teach you how to sift through all of the constant barrage of information to put the best content into the proper perspective that will mater for you and your family.

WealthCycles.com has four different principal sections on the site to help carry out these goals of assisting you to protect yourself and your family from upcoming turmoil and disaster. The Current Analysis section looks at the things that are occurring right now, as well as what the talking heads are gabbing about, and the news that is on the front page these days. This is all done within The Wealth Cycle Principle that it has happened before now and is happening yet again.

The Classic Essay by Michael Maloney proves to be the site owner's essays pertaining to many things. The Wealth Cycle Principle is covered. Other essays explain the ways that these constantly repeating trends can help you to make the best financial decisions right now.

In the Wealth Cycle basics and fundamentals. Maloney and company explain the hardware of this Wealth Cycle principle. This is done so that you will understand the economic cycles and how to react to them properly.

Finally, there are the Tools and Tips to help you secure your Financial Future section. These are how to maps and manuals for those who are inexperienced investors or new to the study of economics. These provide fast reads for the basics and dangers that can way lay even the most experienced of investors.

Recommended Books

The books below are excellent resources if you plan to dig deeper into the history of economic cycles as well as learn more about fundamental mechanics of our current economic state.

If have also included two books on the Fed, which provides you with an even deeper understanding on its founding and operating principles. Remember that the more information you have on your investment the less risky it is. Whenever you feel uncomfortable or even experience fear know that you need more information.

Besides that a few books on this list deal with the mindset, which I think is the most important of all. I mentioned this a few times in the book. Turn your mind into an asset and you have already accomplished 95 percent of what it takes to be wealthy.

And if you like to have a fantastic vision beyond the next ten years you will have a good read on Jacque Fresco's book. He is truly a remarkable man. I share his vision about a resource based society that exists quite prosperously without any form of money.

- Web of Debt by Ellen Hodgson Brown

- Rich Dad's Conspiracy of the Rich: The 8 New Rules of Money by Robert T. Kiyosaki

- Aftershock: Protect Yourself and Profit in the Next Global Financial Meltdown by David Wiedemer

- Debt Virus: A Compelling Solution to the World's Debt Problems by Jacques S. Jaikaran

- Creating Wealth: Retire in Ten Years Using Allen's Seven Principles of Wealth by Robert G. Allen

• America's Money Machine by Elgin Groseclose

• Crash Proof 2.0: How to Profit from the Economic Collapse by Peter D. Schiff, John Downes

• The Creature from Jekyll Island: A Second Look at the Federal Reserve by G. Edward Griffin, Dan Smoot

• Options for the Beginner and Beyond: Unlock the Opportunities and Minimize the Risks by W. Edward Olmstead

• Drive: The Surprising Truth About What Motivates Us Drive: The Surprising Truth About What Motivates Us by Daniel H. Pink [Huh??? -TT]

• The Dollar Crisis: Causes, Consequences, Cures by Richard Duncan

• Life Inc.: How the World Became a Corporation and How to Take It Back by Douglas Rushkoff

• The 2012 Story: The Myths, Fallacies, and Truth Behind the Most Intriguing Date in History by John Major Jenkins

• The End of Money and the Future of Civilization by Thomas H. Greco Jr.

• End the Fed End the Fed by Ron Paul

• The One Minute Millionaire: The Enlightened Way to Wealth by Mark Victor Hansen, Robert G. Allen

• The Talent Code: Greatness Isn't Born. It's Grown. Here's How by Daniel Coyle

• Visionary Business: An Entrepreneur's Guide to Success by Marc Allen

• Empire of Debt: The Rise of an Epic Financial Crisis by William Bonner, Addison Wiggin

• Meltdown: A Free-Market Look at Why the Stock Market Collapsed, the Economy Tanked, and Government Bailouts Will Make Things Worse by Thomas E. Woods Jr., Ron Paul

- The Art of Learning: An Inner Journey to Optimal Performance by Josh Waitzkin

- The Best That Money Can't Buy: Beyond Politics, Poverty, & War by Jacque Fresco

- Rich Dad's Advisors: Guide to Investing In Gold and Silver: Everything You Need to Know to Profit from Precious Metals Now by Michael Maloney (Author)

- America's Bubble Economy: Profit When It Pops by David Wiedemer

- How to Think Like a Millionaire by Mark Fisher, Marc Allen

www.ingramcontent.com/pod-product-compliance
Lightning Source LLC
LaVergne TN
LVHW081534060526
838200LV00048B/2077